PURSUING PEACE

HILLEL

&

MINDFULNESS-BASED CONFLICT

ENGAGEMENT

AN INTRODUCTION & WORKBOOK

BARRY NOBEL, JD, PHD

Pursuing Peace
Hillel & Mindfulness-based Conflict Engagement

© 2018 by Barry Nobel

Excerpts from *Pirkei Avos Treasury* by Rabbi Moshe Lieber are reproduced with permission of the copyright holders, ArtScroll / Mesorah Publications, Ltd.

Cover art: © Bess Nobel

What Would Hillel Say?

If we take Hillel's teachings as worthy of serious study, a second concern arises. Namely, have these ideas been appropriately applied to the conflict engagement model presented here? Two grounds of objection are addressed below: on occasion, the principles espoused here are being applied to very different circumstances; and some of the ancient passages have been lifted entirely out of context.

To support the first practice—applying the teachings in very *different circumstances*—it can be said that Hillel himself was a proponent of adapting laws of Torah to current circumstances.[5] In doing so, he sought to strengthen connections between G?d, Torah (Truth; Revelation), and a changing human community (Israel). He brought people to the study of Torah, while also interpreting Revelation in ways that accorded with Jews' daily lives.

As for the second concern, two lines of reasoning support taking some of Hillel's words and deeds entirely *out of context*. First, this practice mirrors their use in some of the original sources themselves. *Pirkei Avos,* for instance, offers many pithy maxims without providing additional context.[6] Second, extracting phrases and even single words from their familiar surroundings and reading them in a *much broader context* (e.g., of the entire Torah) is a common phenomenon in Jewish scholarship.

Judaism has a long history of adapting sacred principles to current circumstances or ignoring their original context. Tradition tells us that Moses received a written *and* an oral Torah at Sinai. The oral Torah—despite being partially committed to writing more than a millennium and a half in the past—*appears* to evolve continuously over time. According to tradition, Moses himself was befuddled when he was granted a vision of Rabbi Akiba's interpretation of Torah taking place more than one thousand years after Sinai. But the Talmud tells us that *everything* was, in fact, revealed at Sinai.[7] Hence, we are to understand that a multitude of insights and applications emerge from the same set of revelations. Each interpretation must be judged on its own merits, not simply on strict adherence to its original form or context. To repeat: *we are not well advised to blindly adopt the lessons contained in this work or elsewhere. Instead, we are encouraged to contemplate their worth—in light of other esteemed teachings and our own experience—and, if they pass initial scrutiny, then to give them a fair trial.[8] If the trial results are positive—yielding*

---

[5] See e.g., Chapter 1 re: Hillel's creation of the *prozbul.* The practice of interpreting Torah's injunctions in light of their original context is certainly a part of Jewish tradition. But so are the practices of applying laws more broadly to similar situations, as well as limiting broad principles to specified situations. Hillel himself set forth seven principles of Torah interpretation. See Joseph Telushkin, *Hillel: If Not Now, When?* (New York: Schocken, 2010).
[6] See e.g., *Pirkei Avos Treasury* 1:13.
[7] *Menachos* 29b in *Talmud Bavli* (New York: Mesorah Publications, 1996). All Talmudic references are to this version unless otherwise noted.
[8] When should a trial not be undertaken because the lesson fails to pass initial scrutiny? If, for instance, it contradicts other important teachings and/or might well lead to serious harm.

beneficial results for all involved—then we would be wise to continue putting into practice what we have learned from our own experience. Aspiring to maximize good results in this world brings us to consider the mention of the Eternal One in the following pages.

Wondering About the Eternal One

This work makes frequent reference to the Eternal One, more commonly called G?d.[9] For many Jews, these terms and their synonyms don't hold great meaning or worth. Some believe these references are tools of oppression, superstition, or simply, ignorance. This is not the place to treat this subject at length. To appreciate Hillel's teachings, however, it can be worthwhile to keep in mind that Jewish tradition acknowledges that G?d's nature is beyond anyone's ideas. Ultimately, G?d is incomprehensible. Hence, to refrain from defining the Eternal One is consistent with tradition. But for those readers who are put off by this elusive term, employing one or more of the following, related strategies may be of help:

1. *Substitute "Higher Power" or "The Force."* Twelve-Step Programs refer to a Higher Power to be inclusive while recognizing that there are energies at work that are beyond our understanding. Those who follow the *Stars Wars* movies may feel more comfortable referring to "The Force." Ask yourself, "Am I open to the possibility that there is a power higher than, or superior to, my ego? Might employing this concept help me move toward fulfilling my highest aspirations?" It's said that we become more like that which we worship.

2. *Use a concept or description of your choice.* An atheist Jew approached Reb Levi Yitzhak (1740–1810) and declared his disbelief in G?d. The rabbi responded, "I agree with you. That G?d you don't believe in? Well, I don't believe in that G?d either!" It's easy to associate references to divinity with those who have committed great harm. But it's also not so difficult to find examples of admirable people who employed the term to inspire virtuous living.

People understand divinity in a variety of ways. Taken in, perhaps, its best light, divinity could refer to the *highest Good.* Anselm (1033–1109), for example, described G?d as "that which nothing greater can be conceived." Rabbi Mordecai Kaplan (1881–1983), founder of Reconstructing Judaism, defined G?d as "the power that makes for salvation in the world." Salvation, for Kaplan, entails the realization of the full, creative potential of humankind. He wrote, "God is that aspect of reality which elicits from us the best that is in us and enables us to bear the worst that can befall us."

---

[9] In this text, I spell God, *G?d*, and I don't refer to G?d as male or female, except when quoting others. I do this to highlight the mystery to which the term refers.

Why limit our view of the Divine because others have referred to G?d in degrading ways? In other words, why throw the baby out with the bathwater?

3. *Consider your ultimate concern.* Interpreting the term "Supreme Being" in a law that granted exemptions from armed service, the United States Supreme Court quoted theologian Paul Tillich (1886–1965). Tillich wrote:

> And if that word [God] has not much meaning for you, translate it, and speak of the depths of your life, of the source of your being, of your ultimate concern, *of what you take seriously without any reservation.* Perhaps, in order to do so, you must forget everything traditional that you have learned about God. . . . Tillich, The Shaking of the Foundations 57 (1948).[10] [Italics in original]

More succinctly, Bob Dylan sang, "You gotta serve somebody."

4. *Ignore it.* One need not subscribe to any specific view of G?d to derive some benefit from Hillel's teachings and the Mindfulness-based Conflict Engagement model. If you feel averse to the use of a certain word or phrase, use the opportunity to become more aware of your emotions, needs, and values, and then act accordingly. This is a central practice of **MBCE**, as we shall see.

Whatever your attitude toward historical texts and religious language, when it comes to dealing with conflict, additional motivation, knowledge, and skill to engage peacefully and effectively may be of great benefit. To make significant improvement, study is a crucial first step. As Hillel said, "Do not say, 'When I am free I will study,' for perhaps you will not become free."[11] To assist your study, the Workbook contains a summary of many of the principles raised in this text.[12] Yet what good is merely intellectual knowledge in a world boiling with conflict? Study alone is most often insufficient to change deeply ingrained behavior. But, as the Talmud points out, studying leads to *doing.*[13] As a bridge between studying and doing, the Workbook also contains worksheets.[14] These exercises are designed to help you explore your own views and identify obstacles to, and supports for, positive change. It is my hope that completing them will assist you in adapting these teachings to your own circumstances.

---

[10] United States v. Seeger, 380 U.S. 163, 187 (1965).
[11] *Pirkei Avos Treasury* 2:5.
[12] See Workbook, pages 55-57, 61-63, 65-67, 72-77, 79.
[13] *Kiddushin* 40b.
[14] See Workbook, pages 54, 58-60, 64, 68-71, 78.

CHAPTER 1: Mindfulness-based Conflict Engagement: An Overview

[Hillel] used to say: If I am not for myself, who will be for me?
And if I am for myself, what am I?
And if not now, when?[15]

Conflict in life is inevitable. Going a day without a dispute is delightful! But if you think you've spent a whole week conflict-free, you've probably been drifting down an African river—de-Nile.[16] Jews are sometimes considered particularly argumentative. The Talmud asserts that just as no two faces are exactly alike, no two opinions are identical.[17] Bring three Jews together, they say, and you'll get five opinions. When you link differences of opinion with desires for disparate outcomes, you've got the necessary ingredients for conflict.

In a popular tale, a newly hired rabbi quickly realizes that half the congregation stands, and the other half sits when reciting Judaism's central creed, the *Shema*. Seeking greater unity and peace, the rabbi takes the leader of each faction to a long-term care facility to visit Moshe Greenberg. Moshe had been a member of the synagogue's original *minyan*. After introductions, the leader of those who stand during the prayer steps forward and says, "Isn't it true, Mr. Greenberg, that it's customary in our congregation to stand when the *Shema* is recited?" Moshe looks a bit uncertain and replies, "No, I don't tink dets the case." "So," says the other congregant with a slight grin, "The tradition is to sit, right?" Again Mr. Greenberg looks uncomfortable and slowly shakes his head from side to side. At this, the rabbi speaks up. "Mr. Greenberg, you've got to help us out here. The congregation is terribly divided over this issue!" Then, Moshe's eyes light up, and he exclaims, "Ah yes, dets de tradition!"

Conflict is pervasive and persistent. It can bring out the best and/or the worst in each of us, provoking us to develop our divine or our demonic qualities, leading us toward a more perfect peace or dire devastation. When suffering arises as the result of conflict, it may help to recall Winston Churchill's words: "If you're going through Hell, keep going." But we also ought to keep in mind that *if we keep doing what we've done, we're bound to keep getting what we've got*. In fact, one familiar definition of insanity is doing the same thing repeatedly but expecting different results.

A story from the East tells of a horse and rider galloping at breakneck speed, apparently on an important mission. A curious bystander calls out to the rider, "Where are you headed in such a hurry?" And the rider responds, "I don't know. Ask the horse!" The horse signifies our *habits of mind, speech, and body*. These habit patterns—repeated over the years—carry us forward each

---

[15] *Pirkei Avos Treasury* 1:14.
[16] See Workbook, page 54 for a worksheet to explore your own experiences of conflict.
[17] *Berachos* 58a.

Table of Contents

Table of Contents (continued)

INTRODUCTION

Do not say, 'When I am free I will study,' for perhaps you will not become free.
—Hillel[1]

Change is continuous: more people; more technology; more opportunities for constructive and destructive interactivity. More need for creative engagement with conflict! As a mediator, conflict engagement teacher, and more importantly, as a family member and friend, I have come to a deeper appreciation of the obvious: human life holds tremendous potential for helping and/or harming one another. The Jewish tradition refers to the inherent forces underlying such behavior as the *yetzer ha'tov* (the good or altruistic impulse) and the *yetzer ha'ra* (the self-centered, selfish, or evil impulse; the impulse to resist the good). It's up to each of us, on a day-to-day basis, to determine which force gains the upper hand.

In my struggle to be a benefit, rather than a burden, to others, I have learned the most from the practices of mindfulness and Nonviolent Communication (*NVC*). For the past quarter-century, these complementary systems have enhanced my professional mediation practice and led me to design a model for dealing with conflict—*Mindfulness-based Conflict Engagement* (*MBCE*)—that provides the basis for this text. The development of mindfulness—a nonjudgmental quality of mind that focuses on the present moment—is encouraged by all major world religions, including Judaism. *NVC* is a model for peaceful interaction designed and promoted by Marshall Rosenberg (1934–2015). Rosenberg was a psychologist and educator who spent more than three decades traveling the globe to share his teachings on compassionate communication. *NVC* employs empathy and self-empathy to help individuals discover, and work to fulfill, everyone's needs. *MBCE* combines these two powerful resources—mindfulness and *NVC*—to offer a very useful model for dealing with disputes.

The principles and practices described here are not recent inventions; they have been recognized and cherished by Jews through the ages. In this text, I have drawn primarily on the words of Rabbi Hillel and other Talmudic rabbis.[2] Although I majored in religion as an undergraduate, and years later earned a doctorate in religious studies, I am a latecomer to the study of my birth religion. Rabbi Joseph Telushkin's lively works, as well as those of Alan Morinis, founder of the Mussar Institute, helped me realize that, among other profound teachings, the Jewish tradition contains many insightful and practical teachings on conflict engagement. Of special note, Rabbi Telushkin's book, *Hillel: If Not Now, When?* inspired me to write this book.

---

[1] *Pirkei Avos Treasury* (New York: Mesorah Publications, 1995), 2:5.

[2] In this text, references to the *Talmud* include both the *Mishnah* (the compilation of ancient Jewish laws, codified by Rabbi Judah the Prince at the beginning of the third century CE) and the classical rabbinic commentaries thereon (*Gemara*). The Jerusalem Talmud and the Babylonian Talmud were given their present forms in the fourth and fifth centuries, respectively. The latter (i.e., the *Talmud Bavli*) is longer and considered more authoritative.

The present work employs Hillel's ideas to introduce and support the principles and practices that I have found so valuable in my personal and professional life. I hope that you will gain a deeper understanding of how this ancient rabbi's teachings can be of practical benefit today.[3] It's also my wish that Hillel's words will inspire further study of our rich, Jewish tradition, just as they have for me.

I want to address three preliminary questions before concluding this Introduction: "Did Hillel really say and do the things attributed to him?" "If we assume the record is authoritative, whether or not historically accurate, are the principles and practices described below in accord with traditional views?" Finally, "If you have a secular, atheistic, or agnostic outlook, how might you understand references to the Eternal One?"

Hillel & History

If, to film a reality television show, cameras had followed Hillel around Jerusalem two thousand years ago, would they have filmed all the words and deeds ascribed to him in this text? Probably not. Scholars trace some, if not many, of Hillel's thoughts to earlier sources.[4] We also know that it was not uncommon in the ancient world to give credit to a highly regarded individual for ideas arising from various sources.

For our purposes, the fact that Jews have treasured these thoughts for two millennia is more important than historical accuracy. Attributing them to a single source serves to elevate a role model on whom we can focus. It is said that *people follow people; they don't follow ideas*. If this is true, attributing these maxims and stories to a specific rabbi enhances their power to influence us for the better. On one hand, we would do well to avoid blind adherence. On the other, if these ideas pass diligent scrutiny, they deserve to be given a fair trial. And only then, if the consequences of the trial prove positive—yielding beneficial results for all involved—does it behoove us to continue putting what we have learned into practice.

---

[3] More particularly, I am thinking about conflict on college campuses and elsewhere around the BDS (Boycott, Divestment, Sanctions) campaign directed at companies doing business with Israel. Although the BDS campaign is international in scope, creative and constructive engagement begins on the personal and interpersonal levels.

[4] See, e.g., James H. Charlesworth and Loren L. Johns, eds., *Hillel and Jesus: Comparative Studies of Two Major Religious Leaders* (Minneapolis: Fortress Press, 1997).

day, sometimes making our present lives more difficult. But as human beings, we are potentially *free* to overcome past conditioning. We can, for instance, learn to engage with conflict more creatively and constructively in pursuit of peace.

Judaism prizes peace. "Great is peace," an ancient text tells us, "for the prophets have taught all people to care for nothing so much as peace."[18] The teachings of Hillel, the great Talmudic sage, offer keen insight for turning the hardships of conflict into opportunities for the growth of peace. A poor, Babylonian immigrant to Israel, Hillel rose to become the head of the *Bet Din* (House of Judgment) for four decades, until his death in 10 CE. It's said that he was a descendent of King David. Judah the Prince, editor of the *Mishnah*, was one of his descendants.

We could not choose a more apt Jewish role model than Hillel for our study of constructive conflict engagement. Not simply a wise leader and judge, Hillel was also humble, even-tempered, and a promoter of peace. Hillel urged us to "Be among the disciples of Aaron, loving peace and pursuing peace, loving people and bringing them closer to the Torah."[19]

Each chapter in this text uses Hillel's words and deeds to explore our model for dealing with the kinds of disputes we face in our everyday lives—from family and social situations, to commercial encounters, to matters of civic concern. The current chapter introduces the model, called Mindfulness-based Conflict Engagement (**MBCE**). The following chapters each describe one of **MBCE's** four elements, *Mindfulness, Empathy, LifeView,* and *Compassionate Authenticity*. By practicing *Mindfulness* (Chapter 2), we tune into what's happening in the present, highlighting our internal experience, while maintaining a balanced mind. Employing *Empathy* (Chapter 3) yields a deep, nonjudgmental comprehension of others. Enhancing awareness of our *LifeView* (Chapter 4) motivates us to act from our highest values and core beliefs. Finally, responding to conflict with *Compassionate Authenticity* (Chapter 5) expresses our true nature to protect and promote the common good.

Hillel's oft-quoted questions cited at this chapter's outset touch on the four major, interrelated elements of **MBCE**. Before we can be truly *for* ourselves or someone else, as Hillel suggests, we must first seek greater understanding. We must know, as best we can, what is really happening within ourselves (through *Mindfulness*) and with others (through *Empathy*). Mindfulness and empathy yield more than a merely intellectual grasp of the situation. They enable moment-by-moment, experiential insight into what's transpiring. When empowered by a *LifeView* that values *tikkun olam* (repair of the world)—a concept often associated with Hillel—we can act with *compassion* and *authenticity* to meet everyone's needs.

---

[18] *Numbers Rabbah,* chap. 2, section 7.
[19] *Pirkei Avos Treasury* 1:12.

It isn't sufficient to be *for* one and all, only when the going is easy. The most difficult challenges arise when we are embroiled in conflict, and our first impulse is to think only about our own interests. Or sometimes, we don't *think* at all, but simply react automatically and selfishly. These are the times when Hillel's questions above pose the most formidable challenge. These are the times when an experiential grasp of the (***MBCE***) *model* is of highest value.

Two questions deserve our attention before proceeding: First, what is meant by a *model*? And second, why does this model focus on conflict *engagement* rather than conflict *resolution*?

MBCE: Model Not Recipe

MBCE is a model, and not a recipe. In other words, we must *not* apply it *mechanically*. Each of us, and each conflict we encounter, is unique. Consequently, subordinating our intuitive responses to any external formula is insufficient. But I hasten to add this important caveat: as with any art, it's beneficial, and usually essential, to learn and practice rudimentary skills and techniques. In the end, however, we must bring all that we are and all that we know to the situation. It won't do to exalt form over substance. *Technique* is what we use only until the *whole person* shows up.

As mentioned in the Introduction, Hillel viewed Torah as a model rather than a set of rigid commands. He adapted its laws to changing circumstances to foster the applicable, underlying principles. For example, Torah originally required the forgiveness of debts in the sabbatical year—i.e., every seventh year. In Hillel's day, however, the mechanical application of this law resulted in lenders being unwilling to lend as the sabbatical year drew near. To permit and encourage lending and to promote *tikkun olam*, Hillel instituted a procedure to allow lenders to enforce loans beyond seven years. This device, known as the *prozbul,* transferred debts to the court—in name but not in practice—enabling lenders to make loans that could be enforced beyond the seventh year.[20] We're not concerned here with whether the *prozbul* successfully embodied the spirit of Torah. Our point is that Hillel did his best to adapt the black letter of the revealed law to adhere to the spirit of the law.

In this instance, we can see that Hillel was a proponent of the oral law by which the Torah's written law could be adapted to current circumstances. In his embrace of substance over form, however, Hillel was ready to suspend even the promotion of the oral law itself. On one occasion, he agreed to convert a gentile to Judaism even though the fellow rejected the oral law in favor of the written law. Under these circumstances, the sage decided that he need not insist on enforcing allegiance to customary practice. Once again, the spirit trumped the letter. Incidentally, Hillel later attempted to convince the convert to accept the oral law.[21] Accordingly, the flexible use of

---

[20] *Gittin* 36b. Hillel believed that only the rabbinic interpretation of the Torah's law had to be changed.
[21] *Shabbos* 31a.

a *model* for conflict engagement, rather than blind adherence to a *recipe*, allows the confluence of inner guidance and outer circumstance to inform our efforts.

MBCE not MBCR: Engagement not Resolution

The **MBCE** model asks us to concentrate primarily on *engaging constructively with*, rather than *resolving*, conflict. Repairing the world—i.e., seeking the highest good for all—as Hillel sought to do, focuses on the *process* of healing, rather than its outcome. We want to avoid sacrificing the means to the end, even an end as appealing as *resolution*. Zen master and peace activist, Thich Nhat Hanh, expressed a similar sentiment, captured in the title of his book, *Peace is Every Step*. In this regard, Talmudic Rabbi Tarfon declared: "You are not required to complete the task, yet you are not free to withdraw from it."[22] And he urged us to "be aware that the reward of the righteous will be given in the World to Come."[23] In other words, we are advised not to become attached to immediate outcomes. Attachment to specific results narrows vision and increases frustration. Although ultimate consequences lie beyond our control, our *LifeView* can still support our efforts to continuously *engage* conflict with *Mindfulness, Empathy,* and *Compassionate Authenticity*.

In a dispute, to be *for* myself and others could mean rooting for us all—as when I am *for* my favorite team. During a conflict, however, we must move beyond aspiration and take practical steps to assist everyone. But assist us to attain what? In a serious conflict, it's not usually sufficient to cling stubbornly to what I initially think I want. Greater *Mindfulness*, the subject of the next chapter, helps us look more deeply into our own experience so that we can view our interests more broadly. With greater *Empathy* (Chapter 3), we gain greater insight into our adversary's experience and needs. Empowered by clear insight as to our values or *LifeView* (Chapter 4), we can then respond with *Compassionate Authenticity* (Chapter 5).[24]

---

[22] *Pirkei Avos Treasury* 2:21.
[23] Ibid.
[24] See Workbook, page 57 for a summary of Hillel's teachings on the elements of MBCE.

CHAPTER 2: Mindfulness

Make Mindfulness Your Home Base

An ignorant person cannot be a saint.
—Hillel[25]

The bliss of ignorance, if any, is bound to be short-lived. In any event, it doesn't lead to saintliness—i.e., to a strong connection with the Holy One. *To ignore* is to refuse to put our precious attention on what would otherwise be clearly present to us. Why might we be tempted to do this? Two important factors worth bearing in mind, particularly during conflict, are our biases to focus on what's *negative* and to *confirm* our prior beliefs. Let's first be clear about *negativity bias*: it can be life-saving.

To use an extreme example, consider the following. If I go on a picnic in Yellowstone National Park and mistake the sound of a snapping branch for the approach of a bear, running away would be simply a waste of energy. But mistaking the sound of a bear's footsteps for a breaking branch is more problematic: instead of eating lunch, I may *be* lunch. Nonetheless, unchecked *negativity bias,* causing us to overreact to danger and ignore present opportunities, can exhaust us and severely hamper efforts at constructive, conflict engagement.

A second factor leading us to ignore what's present is the natural resistance to learning anything that contradicts our own cherished views. It's often comforting—at least temporarily—to retain our habitual outlook rather than face the challenge of adjusting to a competing, current reality. Because of this *confirmation bias,* we consistently turn our attention to things that corroborate our beliefs and ignore, reject, devalue, or forget that which contradicts our views. As just described, beliefs about those with whom we are in conflict are often negative. Wariness may well be warranted, but so is an openness to new possibilities. Countering negativity and confirmation biases by paying careful attention to what's really going on can be invaluable. Chapter 3 returns to this topic when dealing with the development of empathy.

Mindfulness opposes our tendency to ignore what's present. It entails the intention to be aware of our experience on a moment-by-moment basis, while suspending judgment.[26] For most of us, it's not easy to remember to be mindful. But with diligent practice, it can lead to the growth of greater mental balance and insight.

Mindfulness is the home base of Mindfulness-based Conflict Engagement. The good news is that we're always welcome at this home, and it's never more than a breath away! But it's a

---

[25] *Pirkei Avot* 2:5 in Telushkin, *Hillel,* 204.
[26] Jon Kabat Zinn, *Wherever You Go There You Are* (New York: Hyperion, 1994), 4.

challenging practice as well. In times of conflict, we can act *meshugge*. We automatically react defensively and offensively. We delude ourselves and conclude—without dispassionate examination—that we're right and our adversaries are wrong! Increasing our mindfulness requires the courage to look closely at what's going on around and inside ourselves. It isn't easy to keep the mind open, to look past appearances, to practice patience in the face of strong emotion, and to bring greater balance to the mind. But Hillel's teachings encourage us to follow this very course.[27]

Appreciate the Present

> *But Hillel the Elder had a different trait, for all his works were for the sake of heaven, for it is said: 'Blessed is the Lord, day by day.'*[28]

The ancient rabbis concluded that the line from Psalms, "Blessed be G?d day by day," well described Hillel's approach to life.[29] He trusted and appreciated what the present offered, rather than being overly concerned with what tomorrow might bring. In making the distinction quoted above, the Talmud is referring to the fact that Hillel and Shammai (50 BCE–30 CE) were not alike in preparing for the Sabbath. As the week progressed, Shammai would set aside the most delectable food so that he could enjoy it on Shabbat. Hillel had a *different trait*. Each day, he gratefully consumed whatever food was available.

Life transpires only in the present. To be centered in the present allows us to make the best use of the blessings (e.g., resources) that are available right now. A mindful approach to conflict doesn't *dwell* on the past or *ignore* the future. Rather, it helps us *learn* from the past and *prepare for* what's to come while more fully experiencing and appreciating present potential.

During conflict, it's of crucial importance to increase awareness of our internal reactions to what's happening around us. Mindfulness acts as an *early warning system*, alerting us to both external and internal dangers that might drag us off course. Additional advantages of mindfulness are explored below.

---

[27] See Workbook, pages 55-56, 72-75, 77 for a summary of mindfulness, as well as tips on its practice & application to conflict engagement.
[28] *Beitzah* 16a quoting *Ps.* 68:19.
[29] *Ps.* 68:19.

Maintain an Open Mind, Cultivating Curiosity

Do not be too sure of yourself until the day of your death.
—Hillel[30]

To be mindful is to maintain a *beginner's mind* that is open to, and curious about, reality as it changes each moment.[31] New information and insight are welcome in a beginner's mind, whereas an expert's mind tends to be weighed down and closed off by views previously acquired. The great, twentieth-century theologian Abraham Joshua Heschel (1907–1972) declared that Judaism begins with awe, rather than faith. And awe itself begins with openness and curiosity. A beginner's mind is neither puffed up with pride nor shrunken with shame. The faith that springs from openness and awe is strengthened and made more flexible by an absence of certainty rather than calcified by an absence of doubt.

Curiosity motivates learning. But when conflict arises, and the future appears threatening, curiosity must be consciously cultivated. Asking questions of one's adversary from a place of sincere interest, rather than to prove a point, is particularly helpful. We thereby receive more information, demonstrate regard for the other, and gain time to balance strong emotion with thoughtful reflection. "The question of a wise man is half of wisdom," the poet Shlomo ibn Gabirol (1021–1058) wrote.[32]

Constructive conflict engagement entails two primary phases: *understanding* and *designing*. In the first phase, the most important steps are to understand oneself and others, to feel understood, and to understand the situation more fully. In the second phase, disputants build on increased knowledge and trust to design mutually acceptable ways forward. Although distinct, these stages may alternate throughout the engagement.

When seeking to understand others, it's helpful to regard them as teachers, i.e., as people who can teach us about their point of view. The Talmud's advice to "appoint a teacher for yourself,"[33] hints at the effort required to put someone in this role. It's never harder to motivate ourselves to do this than when we consider appointing an adversary!

Mindfulness enables us to recognize, and move beyond, our own resistance to learning from another. It gives us strength to look more deeply, recognizing that we have an unlimited capacity to learn. In conflict, I'm very likely to make snap judgments about why others aren't doing what I want—more on this in the next chapter. But with greater mindfulness, I become aware of my assumptions. Then I can tell myself: "Maybe I shouldn't *underestimate* my intelligence! I actually

---

[30] *Pirkei Avot* 2:4 in Telushkin, *Hillel*, 204.
[31] See Shunryo Suzuki, *Zen Mind, Beginner's Mind* (New York: Weatherhill, 1970).
[32] Alan Morinis, *With Heart in Mind* (Boston: Trumpeter, 2014), 227.
[33] *Pirkei Avos Treasury* 1:6.

have the capacity to learn more!" Ben Zoma asked, "Who is wise?" The response: "He who learns from every person, as it is said: *From all my teachers I grew wise (Psalms* 119:99)."[34] To learn from our adversaries requires patience.

Practice Patience

> *A quick, impatient person cannot teach.*
> —Hillel[35]

Jewish tradition tells us that humans can potentially ascend higher than angels. Why is this so? Angels *must* carry out G?d's will whereas humans have the choice to do so or to refuse. Utilizing this freedom to pursue everyone's best interests lifts us beyond the angels! Conflict provides the challenging opportunity to choose to do good.

When conflict stirs the pot, it's perfectly normal to react impatiently toward someone we believe to be frustrating our desires. The impulse to fight (or, at least argue), flee, or freeze arises spontaneously. We often believe, in effect, "I'm right, and you're wrong!" We want to give voice to our impatience (our *yetzer ha'ra*, our selfish or lower nature), and *make* the other person understand, and then comply with, our wishes. Sometimes just complying—without understanding—is sufficient!

The desire to have our adversary understand our position is quite natural. We all have a need for empathy at times (see Chapter 3). But acting impatiently is so often counter-productive! It interferes with our ability to communicate what we want. As Hillel pointed out, "a quick, impatient person cannot teach."[36] Exercising patience and then *giving* empathy increase the chances of *receiving* empathy in turn. The Hebrew word for patience is *savlanut*, which literally means *to bear the burden.* In other words, to be patient is to bear the burden of our discomfort rather than attempting to dump the load on someone else. Aristotle was right in observing that *patience is bitter, but its fruit is sweet.*

With mindfulness of our inner reaction, we can strengthen our higher inclination (*yetzer ha'tov* or altruistic impulse). New possibilities for progress frequently emerge if we exercise patience, restraining the urge to *make* the other side understand. We can respond from our higher values, seeking harmony and *power with,* rather than dominance or *power over,* the other. Instead of reacting outwardly, we direct our energy toward the development of deeper understanding.

---

[34] Ibid., 4:1.
[35] *Pirkei Avos Treasury* 2:6.
[36] Ibid., 2:6.

As noted above, mindfulness functions as an early warning system. It alerts us to the challenge before us and enables us to proceed in accordance with the **Seven R's**: *Recognize*, *Refrain*, *Release*, *Relax*, *Re-center*, *Receive*, and *Respond*. To *recognize* that upset has arisen, *refrain* from outer reactions, *release* hasty judgments, consciously *relax*, and *re-center* ourselves increases mental and emotional balance. We are then in a better position to *receive* input from without and within (i.e., to appoint for ourselves a teacher). Thereafter, we can *respond* most appropriately. A balanced mind can express our higher nature.

Balance Your Mind

> *One should always vigilantly guard his disposition so that he maintains equanimity in all situations. Hillel is worth losing on his account four hundred zuz, and yet another four hundred zuz, but Hillel will not take offense.*
> —Hillel[37]

The impatience that disrupts relationships is only one of many expressions of an imbalanced mind. Fundamentally, the psychological, or soul, forces that must be balanced to attain peace of mind are inordinate *attraction to* what we want and *repulsion from* what we don't want. These impulses disconnect us from our current circumstances, from reality generally, and from the omnipresent Eternal One.

Conflict ensues when we don't get what we want. The more *selfish* we are in wanting or craving something, the more upset we tend to get when it's denied. We are *drawn toward* a specific outcome; we are *repulsed by*—or feel anger, or even hatred, toward—what we think stands in our way. These powerful expressions of the *yetzer ha'ra* imbalance our mind. We feel cut off from a source of value in our life, and we suffer accordingly.

With a balanced, or equanimous, mind, we don't plunge headlong into anger/hatred or into craving/greed. It should be noted, however, that equanimity (*menuchat ha'nefesh* or *hishtavut*) is not numbness. We still experience pleasure and pain, yet these states don't readily give way to extremes. As the Talmud says, a pious (i.e., a saintly or kind) person "is hard to anger and pacified easily."[38] Equanimity is not easily attained. It's one thing to value a balanced mind and quite another to maintain one.

In the following Talmudic tale, Hillel does not permit several, purposefully inane interruptions to his Shabbat preparations to unbalance his mind. One Friday afternoon, a stranger arrived at Hillel's home and shouted for him to come outside. The rabbi dressed himself,

---

[37] *Shabbos* 31a.
[38] *Pirke Avos Treasury* 5:14.

graciously greeted the stranger, and agreed to answer his question. After receiving the rabbi's response, the stranger left, only to return twice more to repeat this process.

The stranger's questions were ludicrous: "Why are Babylonians' heads round?" "Why are Palmyreans' eyes so bleary?" "Why are Africans' feet wide?" Hillel responded respectfully to each question, first acknowledging, "My son, you have asked a profound question."[39] Incidentally, the rabbi's answers also accorded respect to the Babylonians, Palmyreans, and Africans.

After the third interruption, the stranger went on to say that he had additional questions but was afraid that Hillel would become angry. Hillel invited him to continue questioning as much as he wished. Finally, the questioner acknowledged that he was trying to make Hillel angry to win a bet of four hundred *zuz* (which was quite a bit money at that time)! Hillel replied, "One should always vigilantly guard his disposition so that he maintains equanimity in all situations. Hillel is worth losing on his account four hundred *zuz*, and yet another four hundred *zuz*, but Hillel will not take offense!"[40]

Hillel's final remark is somewhat startling. Why would he want to preserve his own peace of mind at the cost to the stranger of the grand sum of eight hundred *zuz*? Perhaps, it's because the lesson he was imparting to the stranger was of such potential value. Note Hillel's advice to the gambler: "One should always vigilantly guard his disposition so that he maintains equanimity in all situations." To put it simply, to learn to avoid indulging in reactivity is of great worth. Surely, in Hillel's vocation as a judge, his ability to maintain a balanced mind was of enormous benefit not only to himself but to others as well.

To refrain from taking offense at others' remarks and actions, as Hillel did in this tale, is an accomplishment both valuable and difficult to attain! A balanced or equanimous mind is not insensitive or oblivious. In fact, unless one's temperament has advanced well beyond the norm, balance entails, as noted previously: *recognizing* as soon as possible that selfish craving or aversion has arisen; *refraining* from giving these forces further expression; *releasing* ill-considered judgments;[41] *relaxing;* and then *re-centering* oneself. These characteristics are fruits of *mindfulness* training. *Receiving* input from deeper levels within oneself is the subject of the next section. *Receiving* input from our adversary is treated in Chapter 3. *Responding* with *compassionate authenticity* is addressed in Chapter 5.

---

[39] For consideration of Hillel and truth-telling, see Chapter 5.

[40] *Shabbos* 31a.

[41] Judgments that arise automatically during conflict give expression to biases and are perhaps best called *prejudices*. In this regard, Dr. Paul Ekman, a renowned expert on facial expression and emotion, describes a *refractory period* after the onset of an emotion in which we cannot access knowledge that would disconfirm conclusions reached under the immediate influence of an emotion. Paul Ekman, ed., *Emotional Awareness: Overcoming the Obstacles to Psychological Balance and Compassion. A Conversation Between the Dalai Lama and Paul Ekman, PhD* (New York: Times Books/Henry Holt and Company, 2008).

The Mussar movement, which took shape in nineteenth-century Europe under the guidance of Rabbi Israel Salanter (1810—1883), promoted practical ways to live an ethical life. Mussar teachings seek to remedy the difficulty of living up to our espoused standards. In other words, its methods are designed to help us practice what we preach. Mussar teachers point out, for example, that it's unrealistic to imagine that we will not experience anger, pride, anxiety, etc. Nonetheless, it's still possible to *distance ourselves* from these painful emotions so that they don't control our behavior. The inner experience of upset also changes as we witness it as if from a distance.[42] Mindfulness is the quality of mind that allows us to witness what's up without overreacting.

Performance of rituals—repetitive behavior with focused attention, intention, and significance—can also make a big difference in altering habitual reactions, such as craving and aversion. We are shaped by the routines we repeatedly perform. Regularly attending to breathing is one widespread ritual for developing mindfulness. Conscious breathing is a common feature, for instance, in Jewish meditative practices. In Hebrew, the word for breath (*neshima*) and the term for a heavenly dimension of the human soul (*neshama*) share a common root.

Breath awareness puts us in touch with additional dimensions of reality. When we become agitated, our breathing becomes more irregular. Conscious breathing can re-connect us with our deeper self or soul, our surroundings, and the *Shekhinah,* the immanent Presence of the Divine. It also helps balance any craving or aversion that has arisen. Current scientific research confirms that mindfulness is an effective treatment for excessive stress and other forms of dis-ease.[43]

When we observe our own lack of equipoise in times of conflict and stress, we can avoid prolonged discouragement by reflecting on two basic ideas. First, we have plenty of company in our imperfect state. Second, *self-compassion* at such times fosters *incremental change.* Regarding the former point, tradition informs us that even a *mensh* like Hillel wasn't always flawless in maintaining equanimity.

The Talmud relates two incidents in which Hillel went so far as to insult others who had demeaned his Babylonian roots.[44] No doubt, it can be painful to have one's origins and/or identity maligned. In these instances, Hillel was apparently unable to *Quit Taking It Personally* (**QTIP**). We can draw solace from the knowledge that even Hillel, a distinguished sage, renowned for his patience, lost it sometimes.

---

[42] See Alan Morinis, *Everyday Holiness: The Jewish Spiritual Path of Mussar* (Boston: Trumpeter, 2007), 105.
[43] See e.g., *J. David Crewell, et. al, "Alterations in Resting-State Functional Connectivity Link Mindfulness Meditation with Reduced Interleukin-6: A Randomized Controlled Trial," Biological Psychiatry, http://www.biologicalpsychiatryjournal.com/article/S0006-3223(16)00079-2/abstract?cc=y=.*
[44] Telushkin, *Hillel,* 16.

In expressing anger on occasion, Hillel is not alone. Under a variety of circumstances, Jacob, Moses, and even the Eternal One, reacted angrily.[45] In some instances—particularly in arousing energy to prevent harm—anger can be helpful. But unrestrained anger can be terribly destructive. The goal in **MBCE** is neither to eliminate anger nor to stuff it, but to bring it to awareness and respond effectively to meet everyone's needs.

One strategy to avoid irrational reactivity is to tune into our own and others' *feelings* and underlying *needs*, as opposed to focusing on any disparaging remarks. (More will be said on this topic in Chapter 3 on *empathy*.) When anger has already arisen, implementing the **Seven R's** is the recommended practice here and bears repeating. First, *recognize* its symptoms. Mindfully observing anger and/or greed as soon as either arises strengthens our ability to *refrain* from harmful reactions. Meditation practices that increase sensitivity to bodily sensations are particularly effective in developing an early warning system. Next, use conscious breathing to help *release* impetuous judgments, *relax, and re-center*. With a more balanced mind, we are in a better position to understand more fully what is really transpiring (*receive*) before *responding* respectfully, honestly, and effectively.

To persevere in the quest for greater balance, reflection on the second point above is useful as well—the value of *self-compassion* to bolster *incremental change*. Ironically, a sincere desire to make changes in our distressing, and sometimes disappointing, reactive habits may fuel impatience. When ill-considered words slip out in the heat of the moment, we may be tempted to judge ourselves harshly. Recognition of mental imbalance during conflict, however, need not cause additional suffering. Rather, we can foster greater acceptance of our troubled state. Acknowledging our current limitations, in this sense, isn't resignation. Along with acceptance of what has transpired comes the determination to practice patiently and persistently to realize incremental change.

In these situations, mindfulness empowers us to *release* harsh judgments of ourselves. Going beyond nonjudgment to exercise self-compassion is highly effective. Self-compassion is the intention to relieve our own suffering. To practice self-compassion, we first acknowledge to ourselves that we're suffering and that everyone—Hillel included—has suffered and/or will suffer in similar ways. We then affirm the value of exercising self-compassion by rousing the intention to relieve our own suffering. These two steps are a potent beginning toward breaking the vicious cycle of self-degradation.[46]

Taking this process one step further, we can also contemplate the notion that our efforts to end our own misery will empower us to relieve others' anguish as well. For example, during a

---

[45] See e.g., *Gen.* 31:36-42, *Num.*16:15, and *Num.* 22:22.
[46] See Kristin Neff, *Self-Compassion* (New York: William Morrow, 2011); Christopher K. Germer, *The Mindful Path to Self-Compassion: Freeing Yourself from Destructive Thoughts and Emotions* (New York: The Guilford Press, 2009).

conflict, I may take to heart someone's hurtful remarks, thus diminishing my self-esteem. In addition to using this occasion to strengthen my ability to **QTIP (*Quit Taking It Personally*)**, I may pray that others with similar self-esteem issues grow in self-compassion. Seeing a bigger picture can lead to relief for us all. Compassion is discussed further in Chapter 5.

No matter where we begin, we can gradually improve our disposition by making diligent, skillful efforts. Reflection and practice are of benefit *prior to* the next dispute, *during* tumultuous interactions, and *after* each episode. In this way, incremental change can be noted, appreciated, and reinforced. Recall Hillel's words, *"Do not say, 'When I am free I will study,' for perhaps you will not become free."*[47] He also said, "There is no comparison between one who recites [i.e., studies] his passage one hundred times, and one who recites his passage one hundred and one times."[48] Diligent efforts will be rewarded for we have an infinite capacity to grow.

In the case of **MBCE**, study includes dedication to the practice of mindfulness. It's of tremendous benefit to set aside daily periods to observe and balance the mind. Mindfulness can also be applied anywhere and anytime. It can be very helpful to pair the practice with routine experiences, like waiting in line or hearing the phone ring. In other words, hearing the phone ring can serve as a reminder to take a few conscious breaths. Ordinary events can remind us to breathe and enter more fully into the present moment. The goal is to practice mindfulness at all times.

The attainment of equipoise is at the heart of a story told by the Baal Shem Tov (1698–1760), the founder of Hasidism. Two of the king's friends are convicted of a crime, imprisoned in a tower, and sentenced to die. To offer them a chance to survive, without undermining the justice system, the king makes it possible for his friends to escape across a tightrope over a deep gorge. If they walk the tightrope without falling to their deaths, they will gain their freedom. One prisoner manages to cross the abyss. The other calls out to him, "How did you do it?" The former shouts back, "I don't really know. When I tilted to the right, I leaned to the left. When I tilted to the left, I leaned to the right."[49] Realizing equanimity through the practice of mindfulness is a moment-by-moment endeavor whose reward is increased freedom.

Cook up the Courage to Look Deeply

> *A bashful person cannot learn.*
> —Hillel[50]

Pushed and pulled, repelled and attracted, the mind is often compared to a monkey swinging through the trees. Mindfulness teacher Larry Rosenberg calls an undisciplined consciousness a

---

[47] *Pirkei Avos Treasury* 2:5.
[48] *Chagigah* 9b.
[49] Anthony de Mello, *Taking Flight* (New York: Doubleday, 1988), 183.
[50] *Pirkei Avos Treasury* 2:6.

doggy mind, continually chasing plastic bones.[51] Plastic bones represent our incessant thoughts, lacking real nourishment, that give voice to forces that remain mostly hidden from us.

To pierce the veil of habitual thinking and balance the mind requires us to summon intention, concentrated attention, and sustained effort. To face reality more fully—particularly during the stress of conflict—also requires courage. Conversing directly with an adversary can sometimes be intimidating. Beyond this, it can be scary to bear, and look beneath, the unpleasant feelings that arise when we examine our own behavior. We may find our actions incompatible with our rosy self-image! The influential philosopher Immanuel Kant (1724–1804) challenged us to *dare to know* (*sapere aude*) the truth. And depth psychoanalyst Carl Jung (1875–1961) warned that "one does not become enlightened by imagining figures of light, but by making the darkness conscious." He added, "the later procedure, however, is disagreeable and therefore not popular."[52]

Two millennia previously, Hillel taught that we must not be timid in our pursuit of knowledge. "A bashful person cannot learn," he noted.[53] Courage enables us to face those aspects of conflict, and of ourselves, that have the greatest potential to fuel individual growth and move us beyond impasse. Albert Einstein (1879–1955) is often quoted to the effect that "no problem can be solved from the same level of consciousness that created it."[54] With greater mindfulness, we can acknowledge our discomfort and use emotional turbulence to generate the momentum to help us identify our deeper values and unmet needs. Conflict provides a royal road to greater fulfillment.

Not being shy to learn about ourselves, about others, and about our conflicts leads us to avoid adopting inflexible views of the situation and of ourselves. Hillel put it so well, "Do not be too sure of yourself until the day of your death."[55] Reality is constantly transforming. We cannot rest on the laurels of old character traits or past accomplishments. Sensitivity and ongoing effort are required to progress. With mindfulness, we remain open to seeing even more deeply into the present. Our quest to pursue peace is strengthened by a courageous faith that enables us to forge ahead in the absence of certainty.

Looking mindfully into our own values and needs is a good beginning, but it's not sufficient to engage constructively with conflict. To make additional progress, we must also look empathically into our opponents' underlying views and motivations. Hillel's teachings in this regard provide the springboard for the next chapter.

---

[51] Larry Rosenberg, *Breath by Breath* (Boston: Shambhala, 2004), 22.
[52] C.G. Jung, *The Philosophical Tree*, Collected Works 13: Alchemical Studies (Princeton, New Jersey: Princeton University Press, 1967), Paragraph 335, 265.
[53] *Pirkei Avos Treasury* 2:6.
[54] Possibly found in Albert Einstein, *The World as I See It* (1933).
[55] *Pirkei Avot* 2:4, in Telushkin, *Hillel*, 204.

CHAPTER 3: Empathy

Mindfulness entails suspending judgment to more fully appreciate what is happening in the present moment. Being more mindful counteracts our tendencies to focus only on what's *negative* and what *confirms* our prior beliefs. Suspending judgment requires us to temporarily create a mental space that is relatively free from craving what we like and pushing away what we dislike. With mindfulness, we learn to know ourselves more fully. But, as a popular expression points out, *if you know [only] one, you know none*.

Empathy shares with mindfulness a nonjudgmental approach to present experience.[56] More specifically, empathy involves entering another's world while bracketing one's own. An empathic response resonates with the other's emotions and views. It searches beneath verbal expression to discern what is really needed. Exercising empathy makes it easier to resist taking others' words in ways that sting us. Consequently, we are more willing to gather additional information and to reframe another's behavior in a more positive light. Hillel's teachings demonstrate an expansive and balanced interest in others, leading to more constructive engagement when disagreements arise.

Release Judgment to Consciously Connect

> *Do not judge your fellow until you have reached his place.*
> —Hillel[57]

When conflict arises, our sympathetic nervous system leaps into action. We automatically react defensively and/or offensively. With mindfulness, however, we *recognize* our internal reaction (e.g., a faster heartbeat, flushed cheeks, etc.). If we aren't in imminent physical danger, we can *refrain* from attacking, retreating, or freezing. It becomes possible to *release* hasty judgments, consciously *relax,* and *re-center* ourselves.

In a more grounded state of mind, we can *receive* important input that allows us to engage more constructively. Using our inherent ability to *empathize*—to enter another's experience—counters the impulse to make enemies of those with whom we disagree. Rather than judging, and distancing ourselves from, our adversary, empathy connects us and lays the foundation for future collaboration. The phrases *connection before correction* and *empathy before education* summarize this approach. Along these same lines, Stephen Covey (1932–2012) proposed his fifth of seven habits of highly effective people: "Seek first to understand, then to be understood."[58]

---

[56] See Workbook, pages 76-78 for a summary of empathy, tips on its practice, & a worksheet to explore your own views.
[57] *Pirkei Avos Treasury* 2:5.
[58] Stephen Covey, *The 7 Habits of Highly Effective People* (New York: Simon & Shuster, 1990), 237.

Similarly, Hillel suggests we refrain from judging another until we have *reached his or her place. Walk a mile in the other's shoes* is a familiar admonition today. Comics point to the evident advantages of doing so: you'll then be a mile apart, and you'll have your adversary's shoes! Joking aside, absent imminent danger, consciously entering the other's experience is usually well worth the effort. Empathy enables us to listen with a new set of ears and to respond more effectively. A Jewish proverb points out that we have two ears that are always open and one mouth that is made to be shut. Hence, we should listen twice as much as we talk.[59] In ancient times, Solomon found that "where there is much talking, there is no lack of transgressing, but he who curbs his tongue shows sense."[60] In silence, we can look more deeply at what's transpiring before we respond.

Dig Deeply to Understand Others' Needs

> *[Hillel] even learned the languages of all the peoples of the world; as well as the speech of mountains, hills, and valleys, the speech of trees and grasses, the speech of wild and domestic animals, the speech of demons.*[61]

We read here of Hillel's ability to understand the languages of all beings, animate and even inanimate. This remarkable achievement alludes to the rabbi's ability to understand the *needs* of his fellow creatures, of entire ecosystems, and even of the dark forces. Marshall Rosenberg, the founder of Nonviolent Communication (*NVC*), defined needs as "resources life requires to sustain itself."[62] In Rosenberg's view, we need more than air, water, food, shelter, and health care to survive. We have social, psychological, and spiritual needs as well. To live a fulfilling life, for instance, we need to be *connected* to others, to be *creative*, and to *contribute* to the greater whole. In learning the language of needs and focusing on others' needs, as well as our own, we come to a deep understanding—both cognitive and emotional—of how to sustain and promote life. Cognitive empathy is sometimes called *perspective taking*. We think about and grasp the other's perspective and needs, temporarily suspending our own view. To empathize emotionally, it isn't necessary to have experienced the same circumstances as the other person. Nor do we have to feel the same emotions. But we can remember having had feelings and needs that are similar.[63]

In times of conflict, listening primarily to identify what others need—rather than paying heed to objectionable remarks and personal attacks—is crucially important. We can thereby more easily refrain from counter-attacking, and we can set the stage for collaboration. The intention to

---

[59] Similar expressions are attributed to Epictetus and Zeno.
[60] *Prov.* 10:19. *The Tanakh: The Holy Scriptures* (Philadelphia: The Jewish Publication Society, 1985).
[61] *Masechet Sofrim* 16:9.
[62] Marshall B. Rosenberg, *We Can Work It Out: Resolving Conflicts Peacefully and Powerfully* (CA: PuddleDancer Press, 2005), 4.
[63] See Workbook, pages 63-69 for summaries, lists, & worksheets re: emotions & needs.

focus on needs, rather than self-defense, enables us to **QTIP** (**Q***uit* **T***aking* **I***t* **P***ersonally*) so that we can connect more effectively with the speaker!

But listening deeply is not enough. Even if we possess insight as to the speaker's needs, additional work is often necessary to close the *communication loop*. We must help the other person to *feel* understood.

Paraphrase & Then Pop the Question

> *[The School of Hillel] studied their own rulings and those of the School of Shammai, and even mentioned the teachings of the School of Shammai before their own.*[64]

During heated exchanges, we're often sorely tempted to refute others' arguments without even hearing them out. Two problems arise from pursuing this course. First, *speed kills*—not only on the highways and in drug-use, but also in communication. Interrupting someone to disagree is like throwing fuel on a fire. Second, unless a third party is making the final decision—as in court or in an election-debate—arguing that "You're wrong, and I'm right," is rarely convincing. There are far better ways to approach accord. When the temperature of a discussion rises, it's helpful to ask oneself, "Would I would rather be right or reach a satisfactory agreement?"

Once again, with mindfulness, we *recognize* our inner reactions, *refrain* from interrupting, *release*—or, at least, suspend—prejudice, *relax*, and *re-center* ourselves. We are then prepared to practice empathy and *receive* underlying messages, focusing especially on what the other person is needing. A further aspect of receptivity—*reflecting*—is warranted, however, before we respond.

After we have invested the time and effort to understand the speaker, we may well think it's high time to share our own views. We may say, "I understand!" before launching into our own side of things. But the problem here is twofold. Unless we first check it out with the speaker, we don't really *know* if we do understand. Perhaps more importantly, we don't yet *know* if the other person *feels understood*. When a speaker feels understood, he's much more likely to listen to us.

Reflecting our understanding of essential points in our own words—i.e., *paraphrasing*—and then *popping the question*—"Have I understood you correctly?"—helps the negotiation progress. If our paraphrasing misses the mark, the speaker will be only too happy to offer corrections. And when the speaker acknowledges feeling understood, by a nod or a word, the *communication loop* has been closed. We have prepared the ground to express our own view and be understood.

---

[64] *Eruvin* 13b in Telushkin, *Hillel,* 119.

Paraphrasing provides multiple benefits. It gives the speaker assurance that the listener has taken what was said seriously. It gives the paraphraser a chance to *re-center* before plunging ahead into uncharted territory. It builds connection between participants. By guessing at the speaker's needs—even if these have not been explicitly articulated—the listener lays the groundwork for designing new ways forward. Finally, after feeling understood, the speaker is much more likely to make the effort required to understand the other person.

The following Talmudic tale accords heavenly worth to the practice of paraphrasing in the context of disagreement.

> For three years there was a dispute between the School of Shammai and the School of Hillel, the former asserting 'The law is according to our view,' and the latter asserting, 'The law is according to our view.' Then a voice issued from heaven announcing, 'The teachings of both are the words of the living G?d, but the law is in agreement with the School of Hillel.'
>
> But [it was asked] since both are the words of the living G?d, for what reason was the School of Hillel entitled to have the law determined according to their rulings?
>
> Because they were kindly and humble, and because they studied their own rulings and those of the School of Shammai, and even mentioned the teachings of the School of Shammai before their own.[65]

Hillel's legacy of kindness and humility is discussed in the following chapters. Here the focus is on heaven's preference for the School of Hillel in part because they studied Shammai's rulings and even articulated them before voicing their own opinions. As suggested above, it's important to first study, or to dig deeply into, others' views—i.e., to empathize—rather than to interrupt and/or express disagreement. Thereafter, it behooves us to paraphrase the other's teachings and get assurance that we have understood correctly before responding.

---

[65] Ibid.

Listening to opinions differing from, and even critical of, our own perspective quite naturally arouses negative emotions. *Five P's* offer guidance for empathic reception:

- *Posture:* Maintain physical and mental openness and attentiveness;

- *Pause:* When upset arises, *recognize* internal reactions, *refrain* from interrupting, *release* judgments, *relax* (e.g., by breathing consciously), *re-center* (e.g., by remembering what's most important), and *receive*;[66]

- *Ponder*: (e.g., Ask yourself: "What questions can I ask to help me understand what the speaker needs?");

- *Paraphrase: Reflect* your understanding in your own words, ignoring insults; guess the speaker's emotions and needs; and then

- *Pop the question*: (e.g., "Have I understood you correctly?")

When the speaker acknowledges having been heard accurately, it may be time to offer a *response*. If we are clear about our own values, needs, and general perspective—i.e., our *LifeView*—our words will propel us toward a mutually beneficial outcome. Before diving into disagreement, an initial response that points out *common values* and *needs* and *identifies areas of agreement* builds a bridge capable of carrying disputants toward greater harmony. Being clear about one's own *LifeView* assists this practice.

---

[66] Question: What is the first step to stop yourself from burning with agitation? Answer: *Recognize* that you are burning.

CHAPTER 4: LifeView

How We See Things & What We Stand For

LifeView denotes our perspective on, understanding of, and underlying attitude toward, life. It's shaped by the values and beliefs that give form to our needs. Our LifeView gives us meaning, purpose, direction, and energy. It prioritizes our actions and balances our own needs and the needs of others. When we are more conscious of our LifeView, we can address inner and outer conflicts with greater clarity and purpose.[67]

A story: three masons are employed building the Temple. The first worker is often disgruntled, believing that his arduous task must continue, rain or shine, six days every week for the rest of his life. The second mason is quite satisfied, knowing that his gainful employment enables him to provide for his wife, his children, and himself. The third mason is at peace, even joyful. He recognizes that he's doing G?d's work—taking care of his family and constructing a place of worship that will inspire others for centuries to come.

Our lives and the lives of others are enriched by efforts that align with our highest purposes. If we truly value constructive engagement with conflict, the frustration and disappointment that inevitably arise along the way won't prevent us from pursuing our highest ideals. The intention to seek harmony and to use difficulties as fodder for growth is a great blessing to all.

Repair the World

> *L'taken olam b'malchut Shaddai* (Perfecting the world by G?d's sovereignty).
> —Excerpt from the *Aleinu*

The goal of *tikkun olam*—literally *repairing, fixing, or healing the world*—provides a *raison d'etre* for dealing courageously and constructively with even the most grueling conflict. This ancient, Hebrew concept has long been associated with Hillel, although its precise meaning and usage have varied through the ages. In the *Mishnah*, redacted eighteen hundred years ago, *tikkun olam* refers generally to actions that promote the common good by avoiding the unjust application of law. A line in the *Aleinu*—which became a daily prayer about seven centuries ago—reads, *l'taken olam b'malchut Shaddai,* and refers more generally to "perfecting the world by G?d's sovereignty." The renowned kabbalist Isaac Luria (1534–1572) emphasized the introspective, spiritual component of efforts to bring about this repair. In modern times, *tikkun olam* is frequently associated with working for social justice.[68]

---

[67] See Workbook, pages 58-60 for worksheets to explore you own LifeView.
[68] See Jewish Values Online, http://www.jewishvaluesonline.org/594.

Hillel recognized that fixing the world is an ongoing process. It requires us to adapt immutable principles to evolving circumstances.[69] We could say that to value *tikkun olam* we must keep our *third eye on the prize,* and our pair of eyes on the situation. How might this prize be more fully described? In one word—*peace*.

Pursue Peace

> *Hillel says: 'Be among the disciples of Aaron, loving peace and pursuing peace, loving people and bringing them closer to the Torah.'*[70]

What is peace? Rather than the mere *absence* of conflict, peace is an ongoing approach to life that recognizes and works with differences while, at the same time, appreciating the underlying unity of all being. As noted above, peace activist Thich Nhat Hanh emphasized the importance of a peaceful process in titling his book, *Peace is Every Step.* To respect different points of view is an essential component of the path of peace.

The *dueling duality* of conflict does not necessarily entail destruction. The roots of the term *conflict* mean *stuck together*. In conflict, we are, in effect, bound to our adversaries. Yet we feel separate and scared, and we're prone to react selfishly. Although conflict may be quelled when one side is victorious, and the other vanquished, win-lose efforts and outcomes most often drive conflict underground, only to fester and re-emerge later in new forms. True peace can prevail if all participants treat one another as integral parts of an organic whole. The Greek philosopher Heraclitus (535–475 BCE) noted that "from differences results the most beautiful harmony, and all things take place by strife."

The Hebrew word for peace, *shalom,* has the same root as *shalem,* which means whole. To be whole is to be united, to function as one. To seek enduring peace, therefore, is to search for a way forward that manifests a wholeness that benefits all disputants—i.e., a pluralistic unity. In Hebrew, the term *shleimut* is applied to the kind of wholeness that recognizes both differences and oneness. True peace entails the search for cooperation, harmony, and the recognition of unity in spirit. This describes the win-win approach to conflict engagement.

Hillel, like Moses' brother Aaron, was an *ohev shalom*—a lover of peace. His advice, quoted above, to both love and pursue peace, reflects the Psalmist's admonition to "seek peace and pursue it."[71] In other words, we are encouraged to seek a peaceful resolution of our own conflicts and to help others do the same.

---

[69] See Chapter 1 with regards to the creation of the *prozbul.*
[70] *Pirkei Avos Treasury* 1:12.
[71] *Ps.* 34:15.

The peaceful transformation of conflict's dueling duality is sacred work. One purpose of the Torah, in fact, is to promote peace. It's written that "Her ways are pleasant, and all her paths are peace."[72] The blessing of pursuing peace is the focus of a Talmudic tale featuring two jesters:

> Rabbi Beroka Hoza'a was often found in the market of Bei Lefet, and Elijah the Prophet would often appear to him. Once Rabbi Beroka said to Elijah: Of all the people who come here, is there anyone in this market worthy of the World-to-Come?
>
> . . .
>
> Two brothers came to the marketplace. Elijah said to Rabbi Beroka: These two also have a share in the World-to-Come. Rabbi Beroka went over to the men and said to them: What is your occupation? They said to him: We are jesters, and we cheer up the depressed. Alternatively, when we see two people who have a quarrel between them, we strive to make peace. It is said that for this behavior one enjoys the profits of his actions in this world, and yet his reward is not diminished in the World-to-Come.[73]

Efforts to attain *tikkun olam* by spreading *shalom* are the expression of a harmonious balance of the *yetzer ha'tov* and the *yetzer ha'ra*. The self-interest of the latter is not obliterated, but it's properly subordinated to the altruistic influence of the former. Such balance fosters the soul's development, expanding its reach, even to the world-to-come. In a dispute, however, we are tempted to allow the *yetzer ha'ra* to predominate. To love humanity and bring balance to the world in the face of conflict, as Hillel encourages us to do, requires that we perceive the light amidst the darkness, recognizing the best in each of us, even at the most difficult times.

Recognize the Best in People, Granting the Benefit of the Doubt

> *Leave Israel to their devices, for if they are not themselves prophets, they are the sons [and daughters] of prophets, and will certainly take the proper course.*
> —Hillel[74]

What's our favorite national pastime? In years gone by, *baseball* might well have been the most common answer. More recently, a growing chorus might suggest *football*, given the popularity of both the professional and college sport. But neither response is correct.

Our favorite national pastime is really the *Blame Game*! Think about it. When life doesn't proceed in accord with our desires—i.e., when there's conflict between what we think we want and what we think is taking place—the most common reaction is to haul out the *blame thrower*.

---

[72] *Gittin* 59b, citing *Prov.* 3:17.
[73] *Taanis* 22a in the William Davidson Talmud, https://www.sefaria.org/Taanit.22a.1?lang=bi&with=all&lang2=en.
[74] *Pesachim* 66a.

At such times, we tend to judge ourselves by our best intentions and then blame *circumstances* for our shortcomings. When others don't live up to our expectations, however, we judge them by their worst actions, and then blame their *character*. In doing so, we are committing a *Fundamental Attribution Error* (*FAE*). Rather than admit that we have limited knowledge and then make the effort to better understand the circumstances involved, we attribute erroneous characteristics to our adversary. Sometimes, we also engage in *projection*. In other words, we project on—i.e., imagine we see in—others unsavory, but subconscious, aspects of our own personalities for which we resist taking responsibility.

An example can make *FAE* clearer. If I'm late for an appointment, I might blame the traffic (i.e., *circumstances*). When someone is late to meet me, however, I'll make an inventory of all the previous occasions when she let me down. I'm then likely to conclude that this person is just unreliable (i.e., I blame her *character*).

We're prone to label others with whom we disagree *Crazy, Evil, Stupid,* or—at the very least—*Selfish.* In other words, we fall into a *CESS* pool of blame. We now think we know why they have disappointed or disagreed with us. When combined with negativity and confirmation biases (see Chapter 2), and projection (immediately above), *FAE* harms relationships of all kinds, running rampant during conflict. Such labeling justifies cutting off connections with others. It provides a rationale for ignoring their interests and treating them poorly. It feeds a win-lose mentality.

Hillel sought to steer us away from the commission of *FAE*. His encouragement to trust in people's inherent worth is conducive to the practice of peace and the search for win-win outcomes. In the quote above, Hillel suggests that it be left *to the people* themselves to resolve difficulties in carrying out their ritual responsibilities. Rather than assume the worst, he reminds listeners that "if [the people] are not themselves prophets, they are the sons [and daughters] of prophets." Prophets communicate with, and on behalf of, the Eternal One and foresee the consequences of actions. Accordingly, we might say that the children of prophets will, at the very least, keep in mind life's underlying unity and have some insight as to the impact of their own behavior. We should credit others, Hillel implies, with the good sense to resolve conflict in a harmonious fashion, consistent with the most important principles involved.

A Talmudic tale describes how Hillel himself refuses to jump to divisive and hurtful conclusions when things at home didn't go as he would have liked. In this incident, Hillel's wife is late in serving dinner to her husband and a guest. The rabbi could have attributed this mishap to some flaw in his wife's planning or general disposition. The text notes, for instance, that he might have concluded that she had burnt the food or that she had let some grudge against him or the guest interfere with her task. Instead, Hillel expresses empathy by simply inquiring of his wife why she had been late in serving dinner. She then tells him that, to honor G?d, she had fed the original dinner to a poor man. She also admits that she hadn't thoroughly weighed the consequences of her generous, but time-consuming, decision. Hillel then comments, "I have judged you with an inclination in your favor."[75]

In many cases, we judge others automatically, and too often harshly, when they don't meet our expectations. Here, Hillel avoided negativity and arrived at a judgment in his wife's favor. Given Hillel's frame of mind, his inquiry about dinner was aimed at eliciting understanding and *connection* rather than division between the two. His empathic stance made it easier for his wife to acknowledge that she hadn't fully considered the consequences of feeding the poor man.

In the following pair of anecdotes, the Talmud warns against ascribing negative characteristics to someone without first fully understanding the surrounding circumstances. In the first case, Rabbi Ashi makes a sarcastic remark about a long-dead, idolatrous king named Menashe. Menashe then visits Ashi in a dream, and Ashi asks the king why, if he was so learned, did he worship idols? Menashe responds, "Had you been there, i.e., had you been living when I was alive, you would have lifted the bottom of your garment and run after me."[76]

In the second instance, we hear that Shadrach, Meshach and Abednego—who were imprisoned in a fiery furnace for refusing to bow down to Nebuchadnezzar's image—would themselves have worshipped idols if they had been tortured![77] Blaming others is easier than empathizing with them or mindfully acknowledging our own shortcomings.

Recognizing the best in people and extending to them the benefit of the doubt does *not* mean having blind faith in others or rashly exposing ourselves to harm. Pursuing peace out of a love for humankind, as Hillel suggests, entails a willingness to elevate others at least to the same level of concern that we maintain for ourselves. If we look first and foremost at *circumstances* to explain our own behavior—instead of denigrating our own *character*—we can do likewise to investigate others' behavior. If we do tend to disparage ourselves in such circumstances, it's never too late to develop more self-compassion. Rather than letting ourselves off the hook, exercising self-compassion clears the path for constructive efforts to improve.

Circumstances are more malleable than character, i.e., shaping future circumstances is often much less difficult than modifying someone's disposition. When we *recognize* that conflict has arisen, we can *refrain* from assuming the worst about others just to protect our self-image and

---

[75] *Derekh Eretz-Rabbah VI.* This tale, as well as the discussion of praise for the bride in Chapter 5, and the tale of the king's son and the harlot in Chapter 6 employ gender stereotypes. Although I believe the benefit of conveying these traditional tales outweighs the burden of perpetuating the stereotypes, I encourage readers to alter the genders as you see fit.
[76] *Sanhedrin* 102b.
[77] *Kesubos* 33b, referring to *Daniel* 3:16.

justify our frustrations. Then we can take the time to discover the relevant facts. Finally, we can consider interpreting the situation in the most positive light that is consistent with those facts.

"When it comes to rationalizing self-interest," it has been said, "everyone is a genius!" The ancient rabbis concur, saying that one cannot see one's own blemishes or impurities.[78] Not without making considerable effort, at least. Leveling the playing field between ourselves and others normally requires us to lift others up and reduce our own self-absorption. The quality of humility, which entails precisely this movement, is the final element to be explored here as part of Hillel's altruistic LifeView.

Value Humility Not Self-Inflation

> *My humiliation is my exaltation, my exaltation is my humiliation.*
> —Hillel [79]

In the controversy noted previously between the Schools of Shammai and Hillel, a heavenly voice declares that the law follows Hillel's rulings. Why? Because Hillel's followers were kindly and humble, and they sought to understand, and then paraphrase, the other's teachings before sharing their own views.[80] In a sense, kindness and humility complement one another: kindness elevates concern for others while humility lowers self-importance.

Seeking to act kindly, however, is a more straightforward goal than developing humility. Expressing kindness and its twin virtue, compassion, is discussed in the next chapter. Here, we explore the more elusive quality of humility. Questions to be addressed include: Why is developing humility so problematic? How can we grow (or we could say, *shrink)* in humility? Does humility contribute to simply appeasing others or to more constructive conflict engagement?

In our individualistic culture, the truly humble individual is hard to find. Hasidic wisdom attributes our lack of humility to the prevalence of back problems today—i.e., no one can bend down that low. More seriously, the lack of humility could be the result of societal forces that extol individual achievement and competitiveness. I may not have to win *every* time, but I *never* want to *lose*! Yet self-centeredness and boasting are still considered unseemly, and humility continues to be hailed, at least in theory, as a virtue.

Making peace between the inclinations to both promote and diminish oneself is challenging. The ego's efforts to *achieve humility*—i.e., to improve itself by diminishing itself—may even be

---

[78] See *Bechoros* 38b referring to the blemishes on one's own animal to be slaughtered.
[79] *Leviticus Rabbah* 1:5.
[80] *Eruvin* 13b in Telushkin, *Hillel,* 119.

self-defeating! For many of us, it's *hard* to resist the desire to win approbation by appearing humble and *easy* to delude ourselves about what we're really doing. "Humility for the sake of approval is the worst arrogance," says Rebbe Nachman of Breslov (1772–1810).

Using humor to puncture false humility is a familiar Jewish response to the paradoxical quest to become humble. In a classic anecdote, Israeli Prime Minister Golda Meir (1898–1978) confronts a cabinet minister who has turned aside praise for a recent achievement. The Prime Minister tells him, "Don't be so modest. You're not that great!"

Rabbis, like politicians, are also popular targets for satire. In one account, an ill rabbi lies in bed, surrounded by disciples. They whisper his praise: "Why, he's as wise as Solomon. . . . He has the faith of Abraham . . . the patience of Job. . . . He's as intimate with G?d as Moses. . . ." As they speak, the rabbi tosses and turns on his sickbed. After the students depart, the rabbi's wife inquires after the cause of his restlessness. "My modesty," complains the rabbi, "No one mentioned my modesty!"[81]

Rabbi Hillel avoided falling into the trap of false modesty and succeeded in reconciling authority with humility. For four decades, he served as the *nasi*, or leader, of the Sanhedrin in Jerusalem. As the chief justice of the high court, he no doubt wielded considerable influence. Those occupying responsible positions are not generally known for their humility. But Hillel was an exception.

Following in Moses' footsteps, Hillel combined humility with assertiveness. Moses is known as the humblest of individuals,[82] but he did not act meekly toward the Egyptians nor toward the Israelites themselves. On occasion, he even had the *chutzpah* to argue with G?d. Nonetheless, Moses displayed humility in not seeking anything for himself alone. Meditation teacher Rabbi David Cooper clarifies that "humility means to be clear, confident, and accepting without pride, self-interest, or ambition."[83] As such, humility has been considered inclusive of all the virtues. On the kabbalists' Tree of Life—consisting of ten stations (*sephirot*) connecting earth to heaven and leading beyond to the Eternal—humility is associated with *Keter* (Crown), the uppermost *sephira*. The Crown receives the flow from on high and transmits it below without distortion.[84]

---

[81] de Mello, *Taking Flight*, 113. In the same vein is the tale of the rabbi who confesses to his congregation on the high holidays that he is really nothing and nobody. The congregation is taken aback. The assistant rabbi follows suit, claiming to be even less than his colleague. Again, the congregation is stunned. Then the janitor steps forward and asserts that he is less than the dust under their feet. At this, the senior rabbi turns to his assistant and whispers, "Look who thinks he's a nobody!" Rosenberg, *Living in the Light of Death: On the Art of Being Truly Alive* (Boston: Shambhala Publications, 2000), 153.

[82] See *Num.* 12:3.

[83] David Cooper, *God is a Verb: Kabbalah and the Practice of Mystical Judaism* (New York: Riverhead Books, 1997), 212.

[84] Moses Cordovero in Daniel C. Matt, *The Essential Kabbalah* (San Francisco: HarperCollins Publishers, 1983), 84.

Hillel understood that acting with true humility is empowering, whereas exalting oneself—such as by feigning humility—is the reverse. He said "My humiliation is my exaltation, my exaltation is my humiliation."[85] The Talmudic sages extolled Hillel's example, writing, "Let a man always act as humbly as Hillel."[86] When Hillel died, it is written that the people "bewailed him thus: 'Woe for the humble, the saint, the disciple of Ezra.'"[87]

Although it may be a paradoxical journey, the path to greater humility is not barred to us. To reduce self-importance and avoid false modesty, we can start by acknowledging the tension between the ego and spiritual aspiration. Rabbi Cooper notes that we may begin by mindfully observing moments of self-cherishing. To grow in self-awareness, we can also encourage trusted others to provide us with feedback on our behavior.[88] Humility is the product of a balanced mind, one that is not overly swayed by selfish craving or aversion, nor deluded about its own motivation.

When confronting conflict, humble individuals examine their own behavior and wallow neither in self-inflation nor self-reproach. They don't seek to impose selfish demands on others, nor do they automatically comply with others' wishes. Rather, humility fosters a spirit of both cooperation *and* assertiveness in the search for mutual benefit.

With humility, we recognize more clearly the inter-connectedness of all life. We are willing to cooperate because we neither denigrate nor exalt ourselves or others. We address conflicts with greater confidence, receptiveness, and assertiveness in the service of the common good.[89] It has been said that humility is not thinking less of oneself, but thinking of oneself *less often*. Uniting the interests of self and others is the way of peace. Moses said, "Great is peace, for it is granted to the humble."

A *Mindful* and *Empathic* inquiry into the circumstances of a dispute, fueled by a *LifeView* that values healing, harmony, positive regard for others, and humility, may not resolve every dispute. Adopting this approach, however, increases the likelihood of attaining mutually beneficial results. In other words, a win-win perspective is not guaranteed to succeed. But with surprising frequency, it will surpass win-lose strategies in leading to better outcomes for everyone. The following chapter looks at profound, but pragmatic, guidelines to engage in conflict with both *Compassion* and *Authenticity* to serve the best interests of one and all.

---

[85] *Leviticus Rabbah* 1:5.
[86] *Shabbat* 30b. This line has also been rendered, "A person should always be patient like Hillel."
[87] Adolph Buchler, *Types of Jewish-Palestinian Piety from 70 B.C.E. to 60 C.E.: The Ancient Pious Men* (London: Jews' College Publications No. 8, 1922), 9.
[88] Cooper, *God is a Verb,* 212. The most effective feedback is respectful as well as honest. See Chapter 5.
[89] See Sheldon Lewis, *Torah of Reconciliation* (Jerusalem, Gefen Publishing House, 2015), 233.

CHAPTER 5: Compassionate Authenticity

Engage Compassionately: Do No Harm & Relieve Suffering

> *There was another incident involving a certain gentile who came before Shammai and said to him: 'Convert me to Judaism on condition that you will teach me the entire Torah while I stand on one foot.' Upon hearing these words, Shammai pushed [the person] away with the ruler he was holding in his hand. Undeterred, [the gentile] came before Hillel and presented him with the same request, and [Hillel] converted him. Before the conversion, [Hillel] said to him: 'That which is hateful to you, do not do to your fellow; this, in a few words, is the entire Torah; all the rest is an elaboration of this one central point. Now, go and learn it.'* [90]

The challenge of becoming more fully human may be abbreviated simply as a movement from *SSS* to *CCCCC*. As a toddler, we begin to feel that we are *Separate* from our mother and from all else in the world. This sense of separation leaves us *Scared,* and we react *Selfishly* to defend ourselves and make our individual way in life. At their best, our families and communities help us move from feeling separate to *Consciously Connecting,* from scared *to Courageously Creating,* and from selfish to *Compassionately Contributing* to others. For Jews, Torah charts the course from *SSS* to *CCCCC.*

When the presumptuous, prospective convert described in the incident above demanded to learn the entire Torah in one sitting (or standing), Shammai chased him away. Hillel, however, was willing to meet the student where he was at. To initiate the conversion, the rabbi tells the seeker to embrace what has been called the *Silver Rule*, i.e., to refrain from doing to others what he would not want done to him.

Hillel's offer of brief therapy is surely no complete cure, but it's an invaluable first step—taken, in this case, on one foot. In responding affirmatively to the convert's request, Hillel gave him the benefit of any doubt. Rather than driving the fellow off or demanding that he commit himself more fully before conversion, Hillel compassionately offered him a precious pearl of wisdom to motivate further learning. He then urged the individual not to delay, but to *now go and learn* more.

In negotiations, offering others what is easy to give, but of significant value to them, generates positive movement. The Talmud encourages us to stretch ourselves to assist an adversary, saying, "if one's friend's animal is lying under its burden and needs to be unloaded, and one's enemy's animal needs to be loaded, it is a *mitzvah* [i.e., a sacred duty] for one to assist one's enemy's

---

[90] *Shabbos* 31a.

animal, in order to subdue one's evil inclination."[91] Unselfish action opens the hearts of giver and receiver alike.

Hillel's summary of the *whole Torah*—i.e., to refrain from actions towards others that would be distasteful or hurtful if directed at oneself—is easy to recite, but of inestimable value to those who put it into practice. Practicing the Silver Rule strengthens both mindfulness ("How do I feel when someone does this to me?") and empathy ("How might the other feel?"). Seeing reality through another's eyes—i.e., cognitive empathy or *perspective taking*—helps us refrain from harmful reactions and moves us toward a win-win mentality.

In the heat of conflict, we're prone to believe the best about our own motives. We generally assume our intention is to act fairly. We don't pause to consider how our actions might be perceived by others. But it's my adversary's perception of my behavior—i.e., the perceived *impact* of my behavior—rather than my *intention*, that matters most to her. Before we act, the Silver Rule would have us ask ourselves, "How might my adversary perceive the impact of what I'm about to do?"

The Silver Rule, to *do no harm*, is the negative corollary of the *Golden Rule*, to *do good* (i.e., by treating others as we would want to be treated). The Golden Rule has two closely related components: to relieve suffering; and to promote well-being. In other words, the rule encourages both *compassionate* behavior to relieve suffering and *kind* action to foster well-being, or *eudaimonia*. If we visualize a vertical scale of subjective experience from intense pain and suffering at ground zero to *eudaimonia* in the heavens above, acts of both compassion and kindness move us upward.

Recall the tale in which the Schools of Hillel and Shammai espouse different viewpoints, both of which are considered the words of the living G?d. But the law was in accord with the School of Hillel because, first of all, "they were *kindly*."[92] Hillel's treatment of the convert demonstrates his kindness and compassion. No direct mention is made of the seeker's suffering. But it probably wasn't pleasant to receive Shammai's blow and rebuff, and it's reasonable to assume that something was already amiss in this man's life. Why else would he have approached Shammai in the first place? And why else would he have persevered after that rabbi's harsh rebuke? Clearly, Hillel's compassionate response was intended to help the seeker move up the scale from suffering toward *eudaimonia*.

The Torah offers relevant guidance on what it means to relieve suffering. In short, it advises us to meet others' needs. It reads, "Lend him sufficient for his need in that which he wanteth."[93]

---

[91] *Bava Metzia* 32b.
[92] *Eruvin* 13b in Telushkin, *Hillel,* 119.
[93] *Deut.* 15:8.

The *Shulchan Arukh,* authored by Joseph Karo (1488–1575), is the most widely consulted compendium of Jewish law. It elaborates on this Torah verse as follows: "If he is hungry, one must feed him. If he needs clothing, one must clothe him. If he lacks housing utensils, one must provide him with housing utensils. . . . To each person according to what he needs."[94]

Food, clothing, and shelter are fundamental, physical needs. In addition, humans have social, psychological, and spiritual needs. These include, for example, the needs to connect with others, to live and express oneself courageously and creatively, and to contribute to the greater good. As mentioned above, Marshall Rosenberg defined needs as "resources life requires to sustain itself."[95] When needs are not met, life is diminished, ultimately to the point of social, psychological, spiritual, and physical death.

During conflict, no matter how trivial the dispute, fear and suffering often arise. Our negative, or unpleasant, emotions (e.g., anger, fear, sadness) serve as signals that needs are not being fulfilled. At this point, the fight-flight-freeze reflex often kicks in, leading to defensive or offensive reactions. We easily fall prey to the win-lose mindset. But another path remains open to those who sincerely seek it.

Discontent is inherent in conflict. As a disputant, we can work to use our own upset to fuel empathy for our adversaries. Whereas acting kindly towards them may initially be too great a stretch, it's often less difficult to rouse the intention to reduce their anguish as well as our own. Compassionate action to relieve suffering springs naturally from a heartful *LifeView* that values work to heal the world and pursue peace. At the very least, we can lay a solid foundation for compassionate conflict engagement by following Hillel's advice to refrain from *listening and speaking* disrespectfully (because we ourselves hate being spoken to in this fashion). To then act affirmatively in a respectful, but authentic, manner leads us closer to promoting the fulfillment of everyone's needs.

Engage Authentically: Seek to Meet Your Own & Others' Needs

> *[Hillel] used to say: If I am not for myself, who will be for me?*
> *And if I am for myself, what am I?*
> *And if not now, when?*[96]

Mindfulness of our own emotional turmoil and underlying needs, *empathy* for the emotions and needs of others, and a *LifeView* that values healing, peace, and humility, generate the motivation necessary to explore win-win outcomes. In line with this outlook, the Torah offers

---

[94] *Yoreh De'ah* 250:1, American Jewish World Service translation. http://www.on1foot.org/text/shulchan-aruch-yoreh-deah-2501.
[95] Rosenberg, *We Can Work It Out*, 4.
[96] *Pirkei Avos Treasury* 1:14.

what Rabbi Akiba considered its *great command*: "love thy neighbor as thyself" (*v'ahavta l'reacha kamocha*).[97] We are not to love only others; nor are we to love only ourselves. Taken together, Hillel's first two, well known questions, quoted above, urge us to seek to meet *everyone's* needs—our own as well as those of others. His third question—"If not now, when?"—reminds us to act without unnecessary delay.

To be for myself, as Hillel suggests, I must uncover my needs and then act to meet them. This course counters the alienation and undue stress that result from living out-of-synch with myself. With greater mindfulness, I gain an understanding of what's happening in the present moment around and within me. Looking within, I can identify unfulfilled needs and access those values that inspire me to take constructive, authentic action. Anticipating his death, Rabbi Zusya (1718–1800) said, "In the coming world, they won't ask me: 'Why were you not Moses?' They will ask me: 'Why were you not Zusya?'"[98] I can learn to trust and follow the still, small voice within. In addition, I can gain the inner freedom to acknowledge upset without reacting destructively.

With mindfulness comes the recognition that I don't always live up to my espoused values. But I can also see that wallowing in self-pity doesn't help me move forward. Self-compassion provides the way forward. If I don't treat myself with compassion when I fall short of my expectations, I will be reluctant to look at my shortcomings. This pattern limits my ability to learn from mistakes. What's more, if I don't treat myself with compassion, I really can't expect others to treat me any better. Hillel's first question—"If I am not for myself, who will be for me?"—motivates me to grow in mindfulness, self-compassion, and authenticity.

But if I am concerned only about myself, Hillel asserted, I descend to a subhuman level. "If I am [only] for myself," he said, "what [not who] am I?" As mentioned above, "to know [only] one, is to know none." We are interdependent beings who have needs to contribute to others and support the common good. In addition to self-knowledge, empathy is required to gain a more complete grasp of life. Empathy empowers us to see our adversaries in a clearer light and to understand their views, emotions, and needs. We can then more easily avoid falling into the **CESS** pool of fundamental attribution errors—i.e., labeling them **C**razy, **E**vil, **S**tupid, or just plain **S**elfish. Instead, we can devote our time and energy to exploring the circumstances that surround their behavior and motives. During our search for increased understanding, we can, as Hillel suggested, give them the benefit of the doubt. Deeper appreciation of their plight motivates and assists us to contribute to others' welfare.

We live in an inter-related universe, but not one in which all differences dissolve into homogeneity. This world is well described as a *pluralistic unity*. Accordingly, it's important to see what we have in common and, in addition, to respect the boundaries between us.

---

[97] *Lev.* 19:19.
[98] Martin Buber, *Tales of the Hasidim: The Early Masters* (New York: Schocken Books, 1975), 251.

Compassionate authenticity requires us to heed our own limitations and those of others. As noted above, the Torah urges us to "lend him sufficient for his need in that which he wanteth." Does this admonition to contribute to others' welfare require us then to cater to every single one of another's—or of our own—wants? Not hardly. For everyone's sake, separating legitimate needs from selfish *greeds* is crucial.

Engage Effectively: Fulfill Needs Not Greeds

> *They said about Hillel the Elder that he once took for a pauper from an aristocratic family a horse to ride upon and a servant to run before him. On one occasion, [Hillel] could not find a servant to run before [the pauper], so [Hillel] ran before him for three milin [about two miles].*[99]

In theory, human needs are universal. In other words, we all have the same set of needs. No single list, however, can authoritatively name them all. In practice, needs arise at different times, depending on an individual's characteristics and circumstances. Of critical importance is the realization that a need may be fulfilled in a *great variety of ways*. During conflict, *understanding* an adversary's unmet needs is a major step forward. Then we can employ our best resources in *designing* constructive ways to satisfy these needs.

Not everything that we believe we want will truly satisfy our needs. For example, I may want to harm someone because I think this person has harmed me. Or I may want a million dollars to compensate for an affront to my self-esteem. Yet satisfying these desires may well lead to further suffering, not satisfaction. Desires are endless. Due to our ignorance, their fulfillment may be unconnected, or even contrary, to the satisfaction of basic needs. Referring generally to an individual with untamed desire, the Talmudic sage, Rabbi Yochanan, observed, "when he starves it, he is sated, and when he satiates it, he is hungry."[100] Distinguishing needs from selfish *greeds* requires discernment. To work to fulfill everyone's needs is *heroic* while the pursuit of greed can be *tragic*—i.e., destructive.

In the story at the outset of this section, Hillel provided a horse for a poor man from a rich family. The rabbi even secured a servant to run before the horse. On one occasion, a servant could not be located, and Hillel himself ran for two miles alongside the aristocrat! This incident raises several questions. Was the rabbi feeding this man's exaggerated desires, setting the two of them up for additional suffering? Was the esteemed scholar in need of exercise? Could it be that Hillel foresaw that his assistance would truly enrich an impoverished soul? Might Hillel's contributions save the man from destructive despair and help him get [off the horse and] on his feet again?"

---

[99] *Kesubos* 67b.
[100] *Succah* 52b.

It's unreasonable to assume that Hillel blindly complied with the other's selfish wishes. We know the rabbi didn't suffer from the delusion that wealth necessarily leads to happiness. After all, he taught that, "the more possessions the more worry."[101] Given his advice for each of us to be *for ourselves,* Hillel might well have been seeking to meet his own, as well as the poor man's, needs. For instance, his actions might have enhanced the pauper's healthy self-esteem and met Hillel's own need to contribute to another's welfare. In commenting on this tale, Rabbi Joseph Telushkin surmises that Hillel was probably helping the rider make a transition to a more sustainable lifestyle. Telushkin concludes that the rabbi would not have encouraged others to provide this kind of assistance on a continuing basis.[102]

Although working to meet everyone's *needs* is saintly, seeking to meet others'—or one's own—*greed* is slavery. Gandhi is often credited with saying that *there are enough resources in the world to meet everyone's needs, but not anyone's greed.* To help ascertain whether an action will meet needs or further greeds, two ideas warrant consideration. First, meeting a need can be a step toward benefiting *all* parties and harming none. Second, as noted previously, needs are general; they may be satisfied in numerous ways. Greed often focuses on specifics. When a desire arises, it's often useful to simply inquire, "*Why* do I—or why does the other person—want this?" By digging deeper to identify general sources of motivation, we can then consider a variety of strategies to fulfill the needs before choosing one that all find agreeable.

A simple example demonstrates the value of identifying needs that underlie specific desires. At a meeting, two participants begin to argue about whether a nearby window should be shut or remain open. When asked why she wants the window open, the first person discloses that she's getting a ride home, and she wants to be able to hear her friend honk upon arrival. In other words, this woman is seeking a clear channel of *communication.* The other person asserts that he wants the window closed because it's causing a draft, and he has a cold. He wants to promote his *health.* When these needs are revealed, numerous strategies may be designed to enhance clear communication and good health. For example, the woman might be able to communicate with her friend via text messaging, or the man might change his seat to move away from the window.

The goal of meeting everyone's needs is surely not always so easily met. But the chances of success are certainly increased when people are willing to make the effort to understand one another and then design mutually satisfying ways forward. We conclude this chapter by examining foundational practices to successfully identify and meet everyone's needs. When we listen and speak to one another as respectfully (compassionately), honestly (authentically), AND effectively (wisely) as possible, beneficial outcomes for all become increasingly likely.

---

[101] *Pirkei Avos Treasury* 2:8.
[102] Telushkin, *Hillel,* 67–68.

Listen and Speak Respectfully, Honestly, & Effectively

What do we say in [a bride's] presence? Beis Shammai say:
'We praise the bride as she is.' But Beis Hillel say:
'In all cases we say that she is a beautiful and charming bride.'[103]

As described in the first section of this chapter, Hillel urged the prospective convert to refrain from words and actions that the seeker himself would find hurtful. In times of heated conflict, however, we are prone to blurt out things we think are honest, before giving them a second thought. "I was only speaking the truth," is a common rationalization for saying something unhelpful, or even nasty. In addition, we may fool ourselves into believing that, "if the other party hears the truth, he or she will see it my way!" But when it comes to successful conflict communication, discretion may be the better part of valor. Caring, restraint, and courage are needed in such charged environments.

Truth-telling, or honesty, is a pillar of personal growth and sound human relations. No doubt, Judaism values truth. Rabbi Chanina declared, "the signet [seal] of the Holy One . . . is the word 'Truth.'"[104] And there are times when speaking honestly means expressing criticism. The ancient rabbis noted that "love unaccompanied by admonition is not true love. . . . Peace unaccompanied by reproof is not peace."[105] If someone is running amok, hurting others or themselves, we have an obligation to act. The Torah makes clear that in these cases "thou shalt surely rebuke thy neighbor."[106]

The pursuit of truth, however, can be delusive and destructive when carried on to the exclusion of other values, such as compassion and peace. The Torah's directive immediately preceding the admonition to rebuke one's neighbor reads, "Thou shalt not hate thy brother in thy heart." In other words, although obligated to point out another's serious errors, we must be emotionally balanced and free of ill will in doing so. Following the command to rebuke comes the warning to "not bear sin because of him [i.e., because of the person rebuked]."[107] This is no small task. In ancient days, Rabbi Elazar ben Azaria observed, "I don't believe there is anybody in this generation who is really capable of giving reproof." The sages explain that rebuking with a warm, calm heart charts a middle course between remaining silent (and thereby becoming complicit in wrongdoing), on one hand, and shaming another with one's words, on the other.[108]

---

[103] *Kesubos* 16b.
[104] *Shabbos* 55a.
[105] *Genesis Rabbah* 54:3.
[106] *Lev.* 19:17.
[107] *Lev.* 19:17.
[108] *Shabbos* 54b; *Arachin* 16b.

To reframe these dangers using the language of needs, we must not stay silent about others' needs or our own—including our need to protect and support others. Nor should we speak-up in an abusive fashion. To remain mute may subject ourselves or others to harm. To speak disrespectfully hurts the listener and increases the likelihood of a defensive or offensive reaction. Taking either approach interferes with designing a mutually agreeable resolution.

The desire to be truthful or honest is best combined with the desires to refrain from harm and foster beneficial—or at least workable—relationships in the search for peace. The rabbis explain that when rebuking another, the left (weaker) hand should thrust the person away and the right (stronger) hand should draw him closer.[109] G?d's own activity in this world provides a useful model. The Psalmist points out that "All the paths of the Eternal One are mercy and truth."[110] Here, mercy may be understood as a willingness to balance strict justice with the promotion of peaceful relations. Note that mercy is mentioned first. The Talmud declares that peace is of such great importance that for its sake, even the Holy One modified truth.[111]

We learn from the rabbis that Aaron, the first high priest of the Israelites, was not above bending the truth to restore harmonious relations. To make peace, Aaron individually informed two disputants that the other was quite miserable and very ashamed of his behavior.[112] The implication here is that each person did not *actually* feel guilty. But hearing of the other's suffering *and* admission of guilt, the antagonists were motivated to reconcile. It's easier to forgive when the *other* person acknowledges wrongdoing first! More to our point, truth-telling took a back seat to Aaron's desire to restore peace.

Recall Hillel's encouragement for his students to "be among the disciples of Aaron, loving peace and pursuing peace."[113] In Aaron's footsteps, followers of the School of Hillel embraced the path of modifying truth to avoid unnecessary harm. They took the position that one should always praise the bride as beautiful. Whereas the School of Shammai said "We praise the bride as she is," the School of Hillel said, "In all cases we say that she is beautiful and charming."[114]

One worthwhile approach to an apparent conflict between truth and kindness is to search for ways to be both encouraging and sincere. Two examples may be of assistance. No matter how judgmental I feel, I need not tell the bride that she is ugly, nor lie and say she is the most beautiful woman in the world. Being authentic, I might say, "You look more beautiful than ever!" Or I might avoid judging her appearance by talking about the way I *feel* and what *needs* of mine are being met on this occasion. For instance: "I feel such joy in seeing you shining and smiling here

---

[109] *Sotah* 47; *Sanhedrin* 107b.
[110] *Ps.* 35:10.
[111] *Yevamos* 65b, referring to I *Sam.* 16:2.
[112] *Abot d'Rabbi Natan A* XII.
[113] *Pirkei Avos Treasury* I:12, quoted in Chapter 4.
[114] *Kesubos* 16b, 17a.

before me. My heart is filled with peace and gladness. I'm so happy to be here, to feel connected with you and your family, and to be part of this wonderful occasion!" Incidentally, if I'm not feeling joy on this happy occasion, it might be time to practice mindfulness. Finding out exactly what's going on for me may not only help me meet my own needs but may also enable me to express more empathic joy on this happy occasion!

During conflict, impulsive reactions—often characterized by the extremes of brash, unadulterated honesty or false flattery—are counter-productive. Rather than fight-flight-freeze reactivity, we can learn to respond by *attending, befriending, and FEND*ing.[115] *Attending* refers to the effort to be mindful of the present moment, particularly of our own, internal reactions. We *attend* to our own, inner reactivity to lock our impulse trigger, self-soothe, and get clear. *Befriending* begins by practicing *empathy before education*, or *connection before correction*. Assuming an open and respectful posture, pausing to ponder the situation more deeply, paraphrasing, and popping the question (i.e., "Have I understood what you've said?") facilitate this process.

Finally, the acronym *FEND* summarizes a practical model for listening and speaking with *respect, honesty*, and *effectiveness* to meet everyone's needs. The term *FEND* is intended to bring to mind the expression *fend for oneself.* But in this context, it refers not to the individual self, but to the OneSelf to which we all belong. The acronym *FEND* stands for: *Facts; Emotions; Needs;* and *Designs expressed as requests.*[116]

A listener *FENDs* for OneSelf by gleaning the **f**acts, **e**motions, **n**eeds, and **d**esigns (i.e., requests) the speaker presents. Distortions, insults, demands, etc. are ignored. This focus helps the listener to *QTIP* (*Quit Taking It Personally*). The effort to *QTIP* is aided by the assumption that my unpleasant emotions (e.g., anger, fear, sadness) are *caused* first and foremost by my unmet needs, rather than by what the speaker has said. In other words, other people are not the primary cause of our own bad feelings. For example, no one else *makes* me mad. My anger arises from my own unmet need—for respect possibly. Adopting this perspective reduces the desire to blame others when we hear disparaging remarks. It helps us shift our focus to meeting needs rather than retaliating.

---

[115] The *attend-befriend-FEND* model was inspired by the stress paradigm called *tend-and-befriend* developed by Shelley Taylor and five colleagues. See e.g., http://www.apa.org/monitor/julaug00/stress.aspx.
[116] See Workbook, pages 61-71 for *FEND* summaries and practice worksheets.

FEND also guides communication to help avoid speaking defensively and offensively. Here's an example of how *FEND* can be used to respond to the acquaintance who was late for our appointment (see Chapter 3):

Facts: State the relevant facts (i.e., what I've seen and heard):

> *"You've arrived 30 minutes after our agreed upon meeting time."*

Emotions: Name the unpleasant emotions that arise from unmet needs (e.g., *mad, sad, scared*, etc.):

> *"I feel irritated and disappointed . . ."*

Needs: Express unmet needs (e.g., to connect, create, or contribute):

> *"because I want to be able to trust and rely on (i.e., connect with) my friends."*

Design: Express a request that is specific, affirmative, and practical:

> *"Would you be willing to let me know why you're late?"*
> OR
> *"Would it work for you to call me in the future if you're going to be more than 10 minutes later?"*

Let's look now at a more complex situation, applying the *FEND* model in a less formulaic, more flexible, way. Yesterday afternoon, your girlfriend Kim said that she planned to study that night for a final exam the following day. But this morning, you ran into your friend Joe, who told you that he saw Kim late last night at Tiny Tavern. She was drinking and laughing, he said, and dancing with someone he didn't recognize.

Your first reaction is to call up your so-called *girlfriend* and give her a piece of your mind. You want to let her know, in no uncertain terms, that you're angry. You want to ask her what she was doing at Tiny's last night when she told you she was going to be studying for her exam. What else has she been lying to you about? And who-the-hell was she with, anyway?

But, on second thought, because you've been studying Mindfulness-based Conflict Engagement, you decide to try a different approach. You sit quietly for a little while, recognizing that you are angry, hurt, and afraid. You treat yourself with compassion, using positive self-talk. You get in touch with the fact that you really care about your girlfriend, and you want to be able to trust each other. You start to wonder what was going on for her.

After you've calmed down a bit, you text Kim, asking if she can meet you for coffee after her exam. She agrees. Later, at the cafe, the following conversation transpires:

Emotions: (e.g., mad, sad, scared, glad, etc.):

> *"I'm glad to see you this afternoon. I've been worrying about our relationship today."* [Kim looks surprised]

Facts: (i.e., what I've seen and heard):

> *"I can see by the look on your face that you're startled."* [Kim nods]

Design: (e.g., requests that are specific, affirmative, and practical):

> *"Can I tell you what Joe told me this morning?"* [Kim: "Sure."]

Needs: (e.g., to connect, create, contribute, etc.):

> *"If I sound more awkward than usual, it's because I really value our loving relationship, and this is difficult to talk about. I want us to trust one another."* [Kim: "What's up?]

Facts: (i.e., what I've seen and heard):

> *"Yesterday, you told me you were going to study that night. But Joe told me this morning that he saw you late last night at Tiny Tavern, drinking, laughing, and dancing with someone else."*

Emotions: (e.g., mad, sad, scared, etc.):

> *"I'm feeling scared, hurt, and, frankly, mad."*

Design: (e.g., requests that are specific, affirmative, and practical):

> *"Would you be willing to tell me what's going on?"*

Kim then tells you that she was studying at the library until pretty late last night, and she ran into an old friend from high school that she hadn't seen in quite a while. They decided to unwind at the tavern. She acknowledges that she had been drinking—just a Coke—and dancing—but not slow dancing. And she had been home by midnight. As you listen empathically, Kim goes on to say that she cares a lot about you and about your relationship. Like you, she wants the two of you to be able to trust one another. She says that she's sad that it sounds like she misled you.

By giving Kim the benefit of the doubt, you've expressed yourself honestly and respectfully, learned her side of the story, and shared expressions of care for one another. Each of you has also given voice to your needs to extend and receive trust in the relationship. If Kim is being honest, your relationship has a chance to grow from this experience.

This example attempts to demonstrate that **FEND** is a model, but not a recipe, for addressing difficult conversations. We must flexibly adapt it to the circumstances. Even when we do so, the listener may take our words and nonverbal communication as a rebuke and then react defensively or offensively. But if we're diligent in our practice, we can respond with mindfulness and empathy. No matter how others react, we can remain open to learn of their plight—i.e., what they feel and need. In Stephen Covey's words, we can seek to understand before being understood.

If my tardy friend in the first example, or Kim in the second example, responds to my **FEND** message defensively, I would do well to *listen respectfully, honestly, and effectively.*[117] A *respectful* listener doesn't interrupt. An *honest* listener is not pretending to listen while actually planning a retort. An *effective* listener goes beneath the words to learn the speaker's emotions and needs.

The **Five P's** introduced in Chapter 3 capture the basics of listening respectfully, honestly, and effectively:[118]

Posture:	I lean in and make good eye contact, without rolling my eyes or crossing my arms;
Pause :	I listen longer, resisting the urge to interrupt;
Ponder:	I **QTIP** (*Quit Taking It Personally*) to consider the speaker's emotions & needs;
Paraphrase:	I restate what I've heard, using my own words; and

---

[117] See Workbook, page 79 for a graphic depiction.
[118] The **Five P's** is a model adapted from the work of Peter and Susan Glaser.

Pop the question: I ask, "Am I understanding you correctly?" And if the speaker doesn't feel understood, I paraphrase again after gaining additional information.

After the speaker acknowledges feeling heard, it may be time once again to express my own views. When we each understand one another, and feel understood, we begin designing creative solutions that meet all our needs.

Above all, **MBCE** seeks to avoid harm, improve the present, and create a more wonderful future for all. Its primary goal is *not* to determine the truth about what happened in the past. Courts of law serve this important purpose; but litigation rarely results in mutual benefit. Disputants need not always agree about the past to shape a future that works well for all.

In practicing **MBCE**, the focus remains on how to design a mutually acceptable path forward. Disputants often want to limit expenditures of time, energy, and money. Accordingly, listening and speaking respectfully, honestly, AND as effectively as possible, leads us most expeditiously toward this goal. The rabbis have said, "Just as there is a *mitzvah* for a person to say words of rebuke that will be accepted, so too there is a *mitzvah* for a person not to say words of rebuke that will not be accepted." What is more, "It is not only a *mitzvah* to refrain from speaking words of reproof that will be ignored, it is an obligation not to offer such words."[119]

---

[119] *Yevamos* 65b.

CONCLUSION

*Any dispute that is for the sake of Heaven will have a constructive outcome;
but one that is not for the sake of Heaven will not have a constructive outcome.
What sort of dispute was for the sake of Heaven?—the dispute between Hillel
and Shammai.*[120]

To paraphrase the title song of a 1961 Broadway musical, "Love makes the world *revolve.*" Even so, it may be that *conflict* makes the world *evolve.* Conflict flourishes on several levels. On an abstract level, conflict (sometimes called *paradox*) arises between principles like justice and mercy. Inner conflict pits the *yetzer ha'tov* against the *yetzer ha'ra.* Outer conflict, our focus in this text, sets individuals, groups, and nations at odds.

Jewish life is fraught with challenge. The very name *Yisrael,* originally earned by the patriarch, Jacob, designates one who *wrestles with the Eternal One.* In each dimension of conflict, a worthy goal is to create harmony with one's adversary without being co-opted. In current, mythological terms, a Jedi knight strives to bring *balance* to the Force, rather than to obliterate the dark side.

On the inner level, the struggle between the *yetzer ha'tov* and the *yetzer ha'ra* is ongoing. The Talmud relates that sages once captured the *yetzer ha'ra* and planned to eliminate it. But as the time for execution approached, poultry stopped producing, and the rabbis feared that all forms of reproduction would cease and the world would come to an end.[121] The message here is that it's not possible to obliterate the *yetzer ha'ra* and its concern for the individual self. Tension between the two, inner forces is a necessary source of motivation in this world. We must strive to harmonize self- and other-interest.

When the *yetzer ha'ra* tempts us to act selfishly, or even destructively, the wisest course is to remain mindful and avoid impulsive behavior. Confronting and subduing the evil inclination can lead to peace. After all, as the Book of *Isaiah* declares, it's G?d who creates evil.[122] The *Zohar*—a central text in Kabbalah, the Jewish mystical tradition—tells the story of a king who warns his son to steer clear of immoral women. The king then hires a harlot to seduce the young man. To his great credit, the son resists the temptation. Consequently, the father bestows great honor on his heir, welcoming him to the inner sanctum of the palace. And "Who was the cause of this honor?" the *Zohar* asks. The harlot![123] What doesn't overcome us can make us stronger.

---

[120] *Pirkei Avos Treasury* 5:20.
[121] *Yoma* 69b.
[122] *Isaiah* 45:7.
[123] *Zohar* 2:162b-163a.

As with inner struggles, outer conflict is not disappearing any time soon. Nor should it. The rabbis tell us that controversy for Heaven's sake will have a *constructive outcome*.[124] What would life be like, anyway, if we all agreed on every single thing? Would it be blissful or boring? Would there be any room at all for diversity, creativity, or growth? At the very least, a world without controversy would be very unlike our own.[125]

In this life, conflict plays an important role. Yes, it can be destructive. But, on the positive side, it can generate new and superior opportunities and outcomes for everyone. Perhaps of greater importance, dealing with disputes requires us to grow in our capacity to recognize and accept differences and to respond in creative, compassionate, authentic, and wise ways.

Rather than reacting with extreme aversion or violence to the conflict we encounter, the challenge is to bring our highest resources to bear. More than two centuries ago, one sage explained that "the Almighty ordained that there must be tension and dissension in the world, but it must be channeled into a positive force. The conflict God created can take place on the battlefield or at the discussion table. This is the choice of man."[126]

The courage to communicate with our adversaries is essential, but not sufficient. Even controversies that are brought to the table may not be like those between the schools of Hillel and Shammai, i.e., carried on for Heaven's sake. "There is only one way to tell whether two people are arguing for the sake of Heaven or for their own sake," Rav Tzadok HaCohen (1823–1900) wrote. "If at the end of the debate they love each other with complete heart and soul, then you can be sure that they are arguing for the sake of Heaven. If the argument results in hate then they are arguing for their own ego."[127] Most often, however, we leave the negotiation table feeling neither love nor hate. How then do we know if we are conducting ourselves for Heaven's sake? "The greatest danger," Rabbi Israel Salanter (1810–1883) warned, "is to believe that your dispute is for a heavenly cause—for then it will endure and endure."[128]

Keen discernment is needed to determine if, when, how, and for how long we should engage in conflict. Study is invaluable in this regard. The sages pointed out that studying leads to doing.[129] "Do not say, 'When I am free I will study,'" Hillel admonished us, "for perhaps you

---

[124] *Pirkei Avos Treasury* 5:20.

[125] *Olam ha'ba*, the world-to-come, is a common Jewish phrase used to contrast with this world (*olam ha'zeh*). But the world-to-come is always coming. In other words, the future brings continual change and the possibility for continual improvement as well. In the sense that *olam ha'zeh* and *olam ha'ba* are present at the same time, the eternal now and the temporal continuum are nondual.

[126] *Drashos Chasam Sofer* Vol.1, sermon for 7 Adar 1794 in *One Thousand Homes of Dialogue: The Pardes Project* (Orthodox Union, 1995), 4.

[127] *Yearos Dvash Lemberg edition* p. 53; introduction to *Or Zaura Latzadik*, teaching 6 in *One Thousand Homes of Dialogue*, 4-5.

[128] Telushkin, *Jewish Wisdom* (New York: William Morrow and Company, 1994), 73.

[129] *Kiddushin* 40b.

will not become free."[130] He further advised us to study without *cessation*.[131] But how can this be possible?

Mindfulness-based Conflict Engagement offers encouragement and guidance to persevere in responding to disagreements with compassionate authenticity. The continuous practice of mindfulness helps us gain insight about ourselves, and the ongoing exercise of empathy yields a deeper understanding of others. Neither practice, however, guarantees overnight accomplishment. It's been said that the problem with us today is that we want to achieve success overnight AND get a good night's sleep.

Self-compassion for our struggles, and appreciation of incremental change, promote peace with every step. Patient conflict *engagement*, rather than resolution, ought to be our immediate goal. Rabbi Tarfon taught, "You are not required to complete the task, yet you are not free to withdraw from it."[132] With our world awash in conflict, opportunities abound to contribute to the cause of peace. Hillel urged us to do so, warning "whoso adds not makes to cease."[133]

---

[130] *Pirkei Avos Treasury* 2:5.
[131] See *Chagigah* 9b, citing *Mal.* 3:18.
[132] *Pirkei Avos Treasury* 2:21.
[133] *Pirke Aboth: The Ethics of the Talmud: Sayings of the Fathers* (New York: Schocken Books, 1971),1:13.

WORKBOOK

Worksheets & Summaries

Let your performance exceed your learning.

Study is essential to learning. But even diligent study and memorization of others' bright ideas are insufficient to develop new skills—particularly skills that run counter to established behavioral patterns.

Beyond study, we must explore our own views and values to gain a deeper understanding of how our current perspective and approach may coincide or collide with the changes under consideration. In addition, practice of new skills is essential. And not just any kind of practice will do. Perfect practice is best! In other words, practice doesn't make perfect. *Perfect practice makes perfect.*

The pages that follow provide summaries of the **MBCE** model and offer opportunities to become more mindful of your own views and values regarding conflict (i.e., your LifeView). Thereafter, follow exercises for you to employ the **FEND** model to practice expressing yourself in ways that are respectful, honest, and effective. From the distant past, the ancient rabbis urge you to "let your performance exceed your learning."[134]

---

[134] *Pirkei Avos Treasury* 6:5.

Worksheet: Getting in Touch with My Own Experiences re: Conflict

*This worksheet is **confidential**, unless you choose to share its contents. If possible, in #1 below, choose a <u>current</u> relationship or conflict that you are <u>willing to talk about with others</u>. Please <u>don't</u> choose the most difficult conflict you are facing.*

1. I would describe a current conflict (or relationship I would like to improve)—expressed as an SFD ("shitty first draft" *a la* Ann Lamott & Brené Brown)—as follows:

2. When I think of the word *conflict*, words or images that come to mind include . . .

3. When disagreements arose/arise in my family, I . . .

4. Conflict with family members means to me . . .

5.   **1. Very often   2. Often   3. Sometimes   4. Not often   5. Rarely if at all**
    Using the scale on the line above, I would describe myself as follows:

        ___ a. I love peace and harmony and go to great lengths to avoid conflict.
        ___ b. I sometimes willingly engage in conflict, but only if I see no other good
              choice.
        ___ c. I like the give-and-take of a good verbal conflict and am not particularly
              wary of getting involved.
        ___ d. I enjoy constructive conflict. My adrenaline gets going and I like to see
              what can come of it. I even seek out conflict at times.
        ___ e. I count on conflict to help clear the air, solve problems, and get us to a
              "different place."

6. To engage more constructively in conflict, I would like to learn about . . .

7. Reflecting on my responses above, I would describe my thoughts and feelings in this way . . .

Reacting to Conflict

1. *Automatic/Impulsive Reaction*

Stimulus   ⟶   Impulse Trigger   ⟶   Reaction
                   (*yetzer ha'ra*)   (fight—flight—freeze)

2. *The yetzer ha'ra in action*

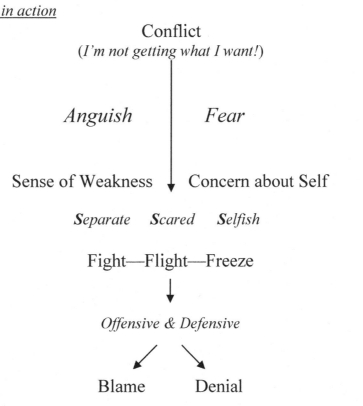

Conflict
(*I'm not getting what I want!*)

Anguish   *Fear*

Sense of Weakness   ↓   Concern about Self

Separate   Scared   Selfish

Fight—Flight—Freeze
↓
Offensive & Defensive
↙   ↘
Blame   Denial

belligerent   contemptuous   critical   defensive   stonewalling

Yetzer ha'ra's **DOBAD** behavior:

Distortion (e.g., *Negativity Bias, Confirmation Bias, Projection*)

Oblivious to emotions and needs

Blame (*e.g., Fundamental Attribution Error*)

Attack

Demand (with threats for non-compliance)

Remedies for Four Cognitive Biases that Feed Reactivity

Bias	Description	Remedies	What Hillel says:
Negativity Bias	What threatens or shocks me (e.g., conflict) impacts me most. *If it bleeds, it leads.*	**Mindfulness & Empathy** *Purposeful, nonjudgmental, present-moment awareness*	*Maintain equanimity in all situations.*
Confirmation Bias	I see what I want to see. *We don't see reality as it is, but as we want it to be.*	**Mindfulness & Empathy**	*Do not be too sure of yourself until the day of your death.*
Projection	I see in others what goes unnoticed in myself (e.g., my undesirable traits). *We don't see things as they are, but as we are.*	**Mindfulness & Empathy** *Walk a mile in the other's shoes.*	*Do not judge your fellow until you have reached his place.*
Fundamental Attribution Error	I fall into a **CESS** pool, considering my adversary: **C**razy, **E**vil, **S**tupid, or **S**elfish.	**Mindfulness & Empathy**	*I have judged you with an inclination in your favor.*

When it comes to rationalizing self-interest, each of us is a genius.

You are not as good as you think you are, and the world is not as bad as you think it is.
Rebbe Wolf of Strikor

Keep two truths in your pocket and take them out according to the need of the moment.
Let one be, 'For my sake the world was created.' And the other: 'I am dust and ashes.'
Rabbi Simcha Bunam

Hillel & Mindfulness-based Conflict Engagement (*MBCE*)
An Overview

Conflict in life is inevitable. Will we *react automatically* to conflict—giving free reign to our *yetzer ha'ra* (selfish impulse)—or **respond** from our *yetzer ha'tov* (altruistic Force) to seek win-win outcomes? *MBCE* is designed to help us maximize expression of our *yetzer ha'tov* & seek win-win outcomes.

1. **LifeView:** *Our perspective on life, shaped by our values & needs*

    Tikkun Olam: "Be among the disciples of Aaron, loving peace and pursuing peace, loving people and bringing them closer to the Torah."

    B'tselem Elohim: "Leave Israel to their devices, for if they are not themselves prophets, they are the sons [and daughters] of prophets, and will certainly take the proper course."

2. **Compassionate Authenticity:** *Acting to fulfil my own AND others' needs*

    Win-Win: "If I am not for myself, who will be for me?
    And if I am for myself [only], what am I?
    And if not now, when?"

    Silver Rule: "That which is hateful to you, do not do to your fellow; this, in a few words, is the entire Torah; all the rest is an elaboration of this one central point. Now, go and learn it."

3. **Mindfulness:** *Locking the impulse trigger & understanding what I need*

    Awareness: "An ignorant person cannot be a saint."

    Equanimity: "One should always vigilantly guard one's disposition to maintain equanimity in all situations."

4. **Empathy:** *Understanding what others need*

    Enter the Other's World:
    "[Hillel] even learned the languages of all the peoples of the world; as well as the speech of mountains, hills, and valleys, the speech of trees and grasses, the speech of wild and domestic animals, the speech of demons."

    Without Judgment: "Do not judge another until you've reached his/her place."

    Paraphrase: "[The School of Hillel] studied their own rulings and those of the School of Shammai, and even mentioned the teachings of the School of Shammai before their own."

57

Worksheet: LifeView

B'tselem Elohim: "Leave Israel to their devices, for if they are not themselves prophets, they are the sons [and daughters] of prophets, and will certainly take the proper course."

Our LifeView is our perspective on, understanding/philosophy of, and actual attitude toward, life based on our values and beliefs. Our LifeView gives us meaning, purpose, direction, and energy. When we are clear about our LifeView, we can face inner and outer conflicts in our lives with a greater sense of purpose.

To develop more clarity about your own LifeView, complete the following survey.

Agree Strongly	*Agree Somewhat*	*No Opinion*	*Disagree Somewhat*	*Disagree Strongly*
1	*2*	*3*	*4*	*5*

Place a 1, 2, 3, 4, or 5 next to each phrase:

____ Life is what you make it.

____ Life is 10% what you make it and 90% how you take it.

____ He who has a why to live for can bear with almost any how. *F. Nietzsche*

____ What goes around comes around.

____ Every cloud has a silver lining.

____ Life is nasty, brutish, and short. *T. Hobbes*

____ I am right now and always, right where I ought to be.

____ It's a dog-eat-dog world.

____ What does not kill me, makes me stronger. *F. Nietzsche*

____ If I am not for myself, who will be? If I am for myself, what am I? If not now, when? *Hillel*

____ Wonder is the seed of knowledge and the purest form of pleasure. *F. Bacon*

____ The universe is not hostile, nor yet is it friendly. It is simply indifferent. *J.H. Holmes*

____ Human calamity is G?d's opportunity.

____ When it comes to rationalizing self-interest, each of us (myself included) is a genius.

Worksheet: Writing a LifeView Statement

Our LifeView Pulls Us Through

What lies behind us and what lies before us are tiny matters compared to what lies within us.
—Oliver Wendell Holmes

Our view of life is shaped by our values. When we become more conscious of our values, we can more easily draw on them for the inspiration and strength needed to resolve our conflicts. Acting on our highest values produces *virtue*.

1. What values are calling for your attention now? Circle 3 that are at the core of your life and 3 that are beckoning for development:

Adventurousness	Family	Loyalty
Assertiveness	Flexibility	Love
Authenticity	Forgiveness	Moderation
Autonomy	Freedom	Modesty
Balance	Freedom	Openness
Caring	Friendship	Order
Clear Communication	Fun	Patience
Compassion	Generosity	Peacefulness
Concern for others	Gentleness	Persistence
Confidence	Genuineness	Playfulness
Consideration	Gracefulness	Prudence
Consistency	Gratitude	Purposefulness
Cooperation	Happiness	Reliability
Courage	Harmony	Resourcefulness
Creativity	Health	Respect for others
Dedication	Helpfulness	Responsibility
Determination	Honesty	Security
Devotion	Humility	Sensitivity
Diligence	Humor	Serenity
Empathy	Insight	Service to others
Equanimity	Integrity	Sovereignty
Excellence	Intelligence	Spontaneity
Fairness	Kindness	Tolerance
Faith	Knowledge	Trustworthiness
		Wisdom

2. Identify an influential person in your life, someone you respect deeply. Name <u>three</u> qualities that you most admire about this individual:

3. Describe what you value in at least <u>four</u> of your most important life roles (e.g., as a son/daughter; husband/wife; mother/father; sibling; partner; employee/employer; friend; student; member of a religious/social group, etc.)

<u>Role</u>   <u>What I Value About It</u>

4. Describe what you now value about how your parents treated you (or what you would have valued but didn't receive) (e.g., being listened to; being allowed the freedom to make your own decisions; firm boundaries, etc.)

5. When you are at your best, what are you like?

6. Imagine yourself at the end of your life. What are <u>three</u> of the most important lessons you have learned and why are they so important?

7. Write a one-sentence inscription about yourself that you would like to see on your tombstone:

8. Write a personal LifeView (purpose/value) statement in the present tense. Let it be both inspirational and practical. (e.g., "I am living fully each moment . . . etc.")

9. Write a personal LifeView statement in the present tense that describes *your approach to resolving conflict*:

Compassionate Authenticity: Four Stages

Acting with *Compassionate Authenticity* includes: being a genuine (*wo*)*mensh*; bringing our whole self to what we say and do to meet everyone's needs and relieve everyone's suffering; making our own, unique contribution to work and to life; being assertive *and* cooperative

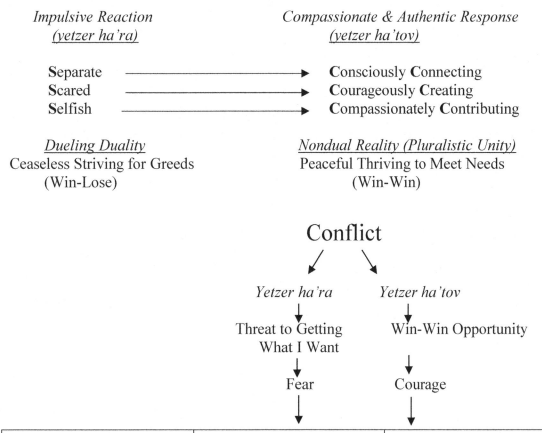

The Four Stages	The Reactive Path	The Compassionate & Authentic Path
1. What is actually happening in this conflict?	Expresses *black & white* *"truths"* as conclusions (**D**istortions, **O**blivious to emotions)	Explores *multiple* *perspectives* focusing on **F**acts & **E**motions
2. What are the causes?	"Your **C**razy, **E**vil, **S**tupid, or **S**elfish motives" (**O**blivious to needs)	Our unmet **N**eeds
3. What is the goal?	To protect or enhance myself (*win-lose*)	To meet everyone's **N**eeds (*win-win*)
4. What are possible steps to the goal?	**B**lame, **A**ttack, **D**emand (& retaliate)	**D**esign a request (with Mindfulness & Empathy)

Compassionate Authenticity: FEND for OneSelf

Win-Win: *"If I am not for myself, who will be for me?*
And if I am for myself [only], what am I?
And if not now, when?"

Silver Rule: *"That which is hateful to you, do not do to your fellow; this, in a few*
words, is the entire Torah; all the rest is an elaboration of this one
central point. Now, go and learn it."

FEND is a *model,* not a recipe. The *intention* to relieve everyone's suffering and to meet everyone's needs must expressed flexibly, based on the situation. Nonetheless, employing certain concepts and using particular language can help to engage conflict with compassionate authenticity.

Language Pointing
toward Win-Win (FEND)*

Facts (what I saw, heard,
smelled, tasted, etc.)

Emotions (e.g., mad, sad,
scared, glad)

Needs (e.g., Connecting,
Creating, Contributing)

Design a Request
(with Mindfulness & Empathy)

Language Pointing
to Win-Lose (DOBAD)

Distortions
(Negativity Bias, Confirmation Bias, Projection)

Oblivious to emotions & needs

Blame (Fundamental Attribution Error)

Attacks

Demands (with threats for non-compliance)

*Based on Marshall Rosenberg, Nonviolent Communication.
(See www.cnvc.org)

Compassionate Authenticity: Facts & Emotions

Facts Lay the Groundwork

Facts attempt to describe reality as it is or was. They describe things or events that we experience firsthand, i.e., by seeing or hearing or, less frequently, by touching, smelling, or tasting. In stating facts, we make effort to avoid drawing conclusions, making judgments, or exaggerating. To paraphrase Daniel Patrick Moynihan, "We are all entitled to our own opinions, but not to our own facts." Facts can help establish a common basis for negotiation.

Emotions Signal Needs

Every moment, our emotions signal our aliveness and our underlying needs. Needs are the primary cause of emotions. Being aware of our own emotions gives us perspective on our experience and helps us to identify our needs and make choices about how we want to respond to those needs. Awareness of our own emotions helps us relate to others' experience more deeply.

Being aware of others' emotions helps us to connect with them, and to understand more fully what their needs might be. When we are aware of one another's emotions and needs, we have a better chance to improve morale and motivation and to cooperate to meet everyone's needs.

Putting emotions into words can help us tune into the enormous richness of our moment-to-moment experience. Talking about emotions can keep them from clouding decision-making and otherwise negatively affecting behavior.

Emotions when our needs are satisfied (not all-inclusive):

Joyful

Happy	Excited	Contented
Blissful	Peaceful	Confident
Satisfied	Grateful	Open-hearted

Emotions when our needs are not satisfied (not all-inclusive):

Scared

Anxious
Suspicious
Worried

Angry

Irritated
Impatient
Frustrated
Furious
Contemptuous

Disgusted

Aversive
Appalled

Surprised/Confused

Overwhelmed
Uncertain

Sad

Unhappy
Discouraged
Depressed
Hopeless

(See www.cnvc.org for a longer list; search "feelings inventory")

63

Worksheet: Get Back to Facts

To resolve conflict, it is very helpful to deepen our understanding of what has been happening and how others see things. This process begins with acknowledging **Facts**—i.e., that which we have experienced (e.g., *seen or heard*) for ourselves. Identifying **Facts** helps us explain to one another, in an inoffensive manner, a part of what we believe has happened and/or is happening.

Instructions: The purpose of this exercise is help shift thinking from conclusions (which often include *distortions, exaggerations,* and *assumptions*) to **Facts**. Rewrite the following sentences using **Facts** only (i.e., what you might have *seen or heard*). For this exercise, feel free to make up whatever facts suit your fancy!

1. You are procrastinating rather than doing the work.

   "You told me that you would have the report to me at noon, but it is 3:00 p.m. and you haven't given it to me."

2. You lied to me about doing the research.

3. You never express any appreciation of my work.

4. All your friends are dead beats and drug addicts.

5. You refuse to include me in your planning.

6. Your office always looks like a pig sty.

7. You got all over my case yesterday. You were out to get me.

8. You broke our agreement.

Compassionate Authenticity

NEEDS are Keys to Conflict Engagement

NEEDS sustain and motivate the physical, social, psychological, and spiritual aspects of our lives.

All humans share the same pool of needs.

All behavior is motivated by needs. Needs are the primary cause of emotions. Unmet needs ⟶ unpleasant emotions.
Met needs ⟶ pleasant emotions.

Some behavior is constructive, or even heroic (when the *yetzer ha'ra* and *yetzer ha'tov* are in balance).

Some behavior is destructive, or even tragic (when the *yetzer ha'ra* prevails).

Identifying our own needs with *mindfulness* and others' needs with *empathy* increases our chances of a win-win outcome.

Because needs are *general* sources of motivation—rather than *specific* desires—needs can always be met in many ways.

Note: To say, "I *need* you to do x . . ." is to use the word "need" in a different way than we are using it in **MBCE** because *needs can always be met in many ways*.

Physical needs include: Air, water, food, etc.

Social needs include: **Connecting**; Loving

Psychological (intellectual) needs include: **Creating**; Learning

Spiritual needs include: **Contributing**; Leaving a Legacy

Compassionate Authenticity

Three Basic Needs

Far Enemy: Too much*	Basic Need	Near Enemy*	Far Enemy: Too little*	What Hillel says:
Controlling	**Connecting** *(Loving)*	Fitting in	Excluding	*Do not separate yourself from the community*
Randomizing	**Creating** *(Learning)*	Producing	Mechanizing	*A bashful person cannot learn*
Self-depleting	**Contributing** *(Leaving a Legacy)*	*Quid pro quo-*ing	Greed-ing	*Be among the disciples of Aaron, loving peace and pursuing peace, loving people and bringing them closer to the Torah*

The Mussar movement, begun by Rabbi Israel Salanter in the nineteenth century, focuses on developing virtuous traits of character, called *middot,* literally "measures." As Aristotle pointed out more than two thousand years earlier, traits must be expressed in the proper measure (i.e., not too much and not too little) to approach virtue.

*The Buddhist tradition identifies the *near enemy* of a virtue as a quality that can masquerade as the original, but it is not the original. The *far enemies* are qualities that arise from an imbalance in seeking to meet a need. Following the Mussar and Aristotelian traditions, each basic need in the chart above is given two far enemies, one that arises from seeking the need excessively (i.e., *too much*) and one from seeking it inadequately (i.e., *too little*).

Compassionate Authenticity: Needs & Designs

The intention to meet everyone's needs (i.e., win-win) lies at the heart of **MBCE**. To help resolve conflict, you may want to use the partial list below to identify your own needs and to guess at others' needs.

Physical: *Corporeal* (to live)

Air, Water, Food, Sleep, Shelter, Health care, Movement, Touch, Sexual expression, Safety, Security

Social: *Connection* (to love)
Acceptance
Appreciation
Community
Emotional Safety
Empathy
Honesty
Respect
Support
Trust
Understanding

Psychological: *Creativity* (to learn)
Authenticity
Autonomy
Beauty
Celebration & Mourning
Growth
Integrity
Play/Fun
Self-worth

Spiritual: *Contribution* (to leave a legacy)
Compassion
Harmony
Meaning
Order
Peace
Purpose

(See www.cnvc for a longer list of needs; search "needs inventory")

Designs Drive Us Forward

Designs expressed as Requests move us toward specific, practical, and affirmative ends. When our designs are expressed to others as *demands*, we seek retribution if they are not met. When our designs, expressed as *requests* or *proposals,* are rebuffed, we use empathy to dig more deeply into the situation so that everyone's underlying needs—as opposed to anyone's greeds—can be met.

Worksheet: Make Emotions Explicit & Nail the Needs

*What might my **emotions** and **needs** be if I had the following thoughts.*

1. S/He's irresponsible; why doesn't s/he let me know if s/he isn't going to follow through?

   "I'm really irritated because my need for order and clear communication in the workplace isn't being met."

2. S/He is so rude sometimes.

3. S/He thinks she knows more than I do.

4. When I ask her to do something, it always takes more time than necessary.

5. Our staff meetings are B-O-R-I-N-G!

6. Is s/he talking again? Why doesn't someone shut her/him up?

7. This is the fourth time she has disrupted our getting together by coming late.

8. S/he doesn't give a damn.

9. I will never find a job.

10. They are crazy/evil/stupid/selfish.

Internalizing the locus of control: Tuning into our own needs—rather than simply focusing on what we think others are doing wrong—allows us to begin thinking about what <u>we</u> can do to improve the situation for ourselves! Identifying others' needs helps us figure out ways (or strategies) that might lead to greater satisfaction for everyone!

Worksheet: Express Designs with Requests

*Imagine that you are tempted to make statements 2—4, below. How might you revise what you are thinking to use Facts, Emotions, Needs, and Designs expressed as requests? Please make sure that your request is **specific, affirmative, and practical** (i.e., can be accomplished by the listener). For this exercise, feel free to create whatever facts, emotions, needs, and requests you feel would fit the situation!*

1. "Screaming abusively at me is not going to get you anywhere."

    Facts: *"When you raised your voice and said I was incompetent,*
    Emotions: *I felt awful, and I got angry*
    Needs: *because I want to learn from you and to be treated with respect.*
    Request: *If my work doesn't meet your expectations in the future, would you be willing to sit down with me and tell me in a quiet manner exactly how to improve it?"*

2. "We have to work together on this project. If that isn't important to you, it's all over."
    Facts:
    Emotions:
    Needs:
    Request:

3. "I am sick and tired of having to deal with the messes you make."
    Facts:
    Emotions:
    Needs:
    Request:

4. "There is no way that I can do what you're asking of me."
    Facts:
    Emotions:
    Needs:
    Request:

Worksheet: FEND for OneSelf

Fill out this sheet to improve a situation at school, work, home, or elsewhere that involves your interaction with one other person.

Name the issue you wish to improve: _____

F – Face the Facts. Describe what you did, saw and/or heard about this issue. (Remember to avoid distortions, assumptions, generalizations, conclusions, and judgments.)

"I saw/heard/did . . .

E – Emotions: What are/were your **Emotions** (e.g., mad, sad, scared, glad) about this situation?

"And was/am feeling . . .

N – Needs: What **Needs** of yours are *causing* your emotions?

"because I was/am needing/wanting/valuing . . .

D – Designs: Express **specific, affirmative, practical Requests** of the other person rather than making demands. For example, "Would you be willing to . . . (e.g., do the following for me . . . (e.g., tell me what you heard me say; tell me how you feel; adopt the following practice . . . .)?"

"And I am wondering if you would be willing to . . .

*Based on the work of Marshall Rosenberg, Nonviolent Communication.
See www.cnvc.org

*Now guess at the other person's perspective (**Facts**, **Emotions**, **Needs**, and **Requests**).*

1. Guess at:

F – Facts: Guess what the other party might have done, seen and/or heard about this issue. (Remember to avoid distortions, assumptions, generalizations, conclusions, and judgments.)

"Did you see/hear/do . . . ?

E – Emotions: Guess the other party's **Emotions** (e.g., mad, sad, scared, glad).

"Are/were you feeling . . . ?

N – Needs: Guess what **Needs** are *causing* the other party's emotions?

"because you are needing/wanting/valuing . . . ?

D – Designs: Guess what the other party might be **Requesting** of you? (Describe **specific, affirmative, practical requests.**)

"Are you wondering if I would be willing to . . . ?

2. Balance: *To attain a broader, more balanced perspective:*

a. List contributions that this person has made to your life:

b. List positive qualities/attributes that this person displays:

c. List this person's other accomplishments that you know of:

The Two Wings of Mindfulness

Awareness: *"An ignorant person cannot be a saint."*

Equanimity*: "One should always vigilantly guard one's disposition to maintain equanimity in all situations."*

To fly, a bird must have two wings of equal size and strength. The two aspects of mindfulness—*Awareness & Equanimity*—must be of equal size and strength for the practitioner to make steady progress.

<u>Awareness</u>

Alert:	Not agitated or dull
Present:	Not lost in the past or future

<u>Equanimity</u>

Nonjudgmental:	Not praising or blaming
Non-reactive:	Not craving/clinging or aversive/hating

Lock the Impulse Trigger

1. *Automatic/Impulsive Reaction*

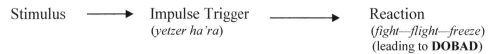

Stimulus   ⟶   Impulse Trigger   ⟶   Reaction
(yetzer ha'ra)   *(fight—flight—freeze)*
                      (leading to **DOBAD**)

2. *Mindful Response*

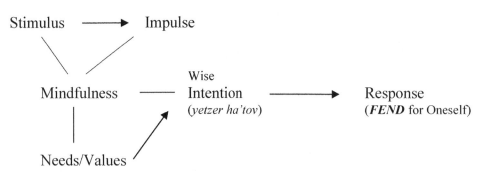

Stimulus ⟶ Impulse

Mindfulness — Wise Intention *(yetzer ha'tov)* ⟶ Response *(**FEND** for Oneself)*

Needs/Values

STOP to Lock the Impulse Trigger

S – **S**top what you are doing (or about to do)
T – **T**ake a few conscious breaths
O – **O**bserve with **COAL** (**C**uriosity; **O**penness; **A**cceptance; **L**etting go)
P – **P**ractice daily to **P**repare! And remember to **P**air with daily activities

Reframe Misconceptions About Mindfulness

Mindfulness means purposefully attending to the present, apart from judgment or impulsive reaction. The following ideas about mindfulness point to the experience of mindfulness; they are not the truth itself.

Misconception #1: My motivation for practicing is to experience pleasant feelings.

> *Reframe:* I practice to get more deeply in touch with whatever I am experiencing in the present moment. This will enable me to change the selfish, often unconscious habit of craving pleasure and running from discomfort. To change this pattern, I remain aware and balanced—neither denying what is present nor losing myself in what is happening (by judging or reacting to it). Ultimately, I believe this practice leads to greater understanding/insight/wisdom, greater compassion for myself and others, and to living a more fulfilled life. If my immediate goal is to experience pleasure, I may ignore what is really happening or get stuck in frustration because I am not getting what I want. This habit will not help me overcome the reactive pattern of my mind.

Misconception #2: I practice to gain extraordinary experiences and powers.

> *Reframe:* My desire to have extraordinary experiences and powers leads me away from what I am really experiencing. Present experience is the doorway to transformation and healing. I enter this doorway to go more deeply into reality.

Misconception #3: Mindfulness practice means that I will never be very happy or sad because I am so busy observing and remaining equanimous.

> *Reframe:* When I am happy or sad or feeling any emotion, mindfulness helps me to experience where I am at, without denying or wallowing in it. I'm not scared of my feelings, and I realize that by experiencing them with an open and balanced mind, I am less likely to get swept away into moods or destructive states of mind. Mindfulness helps me to experience the present rather than hang on to past emotional states.

Misconception #4: Mindfulness is a distant goal rather than something I experience.

> *Reframe:* I can experience an instant of mindfulness right now by purposefully examining my present experience (e.g., my breath), without judging it or reacting to it by wanting it to be other than how it is.

Misconception #5: Mindfulness practice requires long periods of sitting.

Reframe: We can be mindful whenever we are awake. Sitting regularly with eyes closed (e.g., at the beginning and/or end of the day, and/or for briefer periods during the day) is excellent. Less formal practice at other times with eyes open or closed is also beneficial (e.g., before answering a ringing phone, while waiting in line or for a red light). Some people find it most helpful to be engaged in other types of activities while practicing (e.g., knitting, martial arts, etc.). Continuity of proper practice is the secret of success.

Misconception #6: If I were mindful, I would not be thinking while practicing.

Reframe: Thinking is a natural function of the mind. If I realize that I have become lost in thought, I can practice mindfulness by returning my focus to the breath . When I judge myself for thinking, or react with craving or aversion, I have an excellent opportunity to practice self-compassion.

Misconception #7: If I were mindful, I would never recall the past or plan for the future.

Reframe: I don't want to dwell in the past or worry needlessly about the future. But I can be mindful of what has happened in the past to appreciate and learn from it. And I can envision a more wonderful future, considering where I am right now, to make practical plans for improvement.

Misconception #8: If mindfulness means not desiring things to be different, I must choose between getting anything done and being mindful.

Reframe: When impulses and desires arise, mindfulness allows me to identify them and look into them before acting. This allows me to choose whether and how to act based on my higher values, rather than simply reacting based on past conditioning. When I do act, I can be mindful of what I am doing and see the consequences of what I am doing, rather than getting lost in the action and ignoring the consequences.

Misconception #9: If mindfulness means not judging, I will not be able to choose between actions that are harmful and helpful to myself and others.

Reframe: The practice of mindfulness helps me to act from my highest values rather than to react selfishly (see #8, above). Helping rather than hurting myself and others involves: 1) Having a clear sense of my purpose to be helpful; 2) Understanding the present situation deeply; and 3) Taking precise action to transform the present in line with my higher needs, values, and purposes.

The Seven R's of Mindfulness

"Blessed be G?d day by day."

1. Recognize

a. What is present

b. Early warning signs (physical, emotional, mental upset)

2. Refrain from

a. Losing yourself in the past or future

b. Longing for things to be different (greed or ill will)

3. Release

Premature conclusions based on exaggerations, assumptions, and judgments

4. Relax & 5. Re-Center

a. Calming body and mind with
  • Breath, concepts, images, objects, movement, etc.

b. Attaining balance, equanimity, temperance
  • Neither denying nor indulging

c. Letting go; detaching; dis-identifying

6. Receive (Listen/Look) Deeply

a. Being present with an inquiring mind to this changing reality

b. Asking:
  • What am I doing? (breathing, posture, speaking, acting)
  • What facts am I observing? (seeing, hearing, etc.)
  • What emotions am I feeling? (pleasant, neutral, or unpleasant)
  • What am I needing? (distinguish need from greed)
  • What future might I design? (distinguish requests from demands)

7. Respond (with empathy: respectfully, honestly, & effectively)

The Seven R's of Empathy

"Do not judge your fellow until you have reached his place."

Empathy entails the temporary suspension of judgment to gain a respectful understanding of another's experience, keeping in mind that understanding does not equal agreement

1. Recognize

The intention to stand in the other's place (emotionally & cognitively)

2. Refrain from

a. Ignoring, avoiding, or denying (defending)
b. Interrupting, judging, blaming, or attacking (offending)
c. Giving advice or problem-solving
d. Taking what is said personally (i.e., *Quit Taking It Personally*: *QTIP*)
    - Don't listen for conclusions (exaggerations, assumptions, judgments)
    - Translate attacks into requests for help

3. Release

Premature conclusions based on exaggerations, assumptions, and judgments

4. Relax & 5. Re-Center

a. Breathing
b. Assuming a comfortable posture in a safe environment
c. Reminding yourself of your priorities (LifeView)
d. Taking a time-out when needed

6. Receive (Listen/Look) Deeply

a. Know thyself first (i.e., employ mindfulness & self-compassion)
b. Intention is preeminent
    - "Seek first to understand, then to be understood." S. Covey
c. Be present
    - Emptying the faculties
    - Observing nonverbal as well as verbal aspects
d. Seek the underlying reality before problem-solving
    - **F**acts; **E**motions; **N**eeds; **D**esigns (Requests)
e. Take your time

7. Reflect (paraphrase & ask, "Have I understood you correctly?")

Mindfulness during Conflict: Let it RAIN![135]

- **R**ecognize the impulse (e.g., craving or aversion);

  [Level 2: **R**efrain from impulsive action & **R**elax]

- **A**ccept your bodily state (e.g., with a word or nod)
  Don't ignore it, distract yourself, or try to change it

  [Level 2: **A**cknowledge the challenge: Conflict can help me grow!]

- **I**nvestigate the **SEN** of it (**S**ensations; **E**motions; **N**eeds)
  Ask: *"What Sensations do I feel right now?"*

  [Level 2: *"What are my Emotions & Needs?"*]

- **N**ote the experience with a simple word/phrase:
  Sensations: e.g., *"Quivering"*

  [Level 2: **E**motions: e.g., Mad; Sad; Scared; Glad
        Needs: e.g., Connect; Create; Contribute]

  [Level 3: **N**ote with **N**onjudgment; **N**on-attachment; **N**on-identification]

Empathy during Conflict: RAIN for Joint Gain!

- **R**ecognize the impulse to interrupt or tune out

- **A**cknowledge the challenge (e.g., with a word or nod)
  Conflict can lead to growth!
  The other person is doing the best s/he can right now!

- **I**nvestigate by guessing at the other's *emotions & needs*
      Emotions: e.g., Mad; Sad; Scared; Glad
      Needs: e.g., Connect with respect; Courageously Create;
                Compassionately Contribute

- **N**ote the other's reply by *paraphrasing* emotions & needs

---

[135] Adapted from Judson Brewer, *The Craving Mind: From Cigarettes to Smartphones to Love* (New Haven: Yale University Press, 2017).

Worksheet: Empathy—Insights into Reaching Another's Place

"Do not judge another until you've reached his/her place."

1. For me, *reaching another's place* is about . . .

2. It's also about . . .

3. I am comfortable reaching another's place when . . .

4. I am <u>not</u> comfortable reaching another's place (e.g., in a conflict) when . . .

5. Reaching another's place is <u>not</u> about . . .

6. An important thing about reaching another's place (e.g., in a conflict) is . . .

7. Listening to others (e.g., during a conflict) . . .

8. I have the courage to . . .

9. Others can support me as I attempt to reach another's place by . . .

10. Reviewing my responses above, I feel/think . . .

Listen & Speak

Respectfully, Honestly, & Effectively

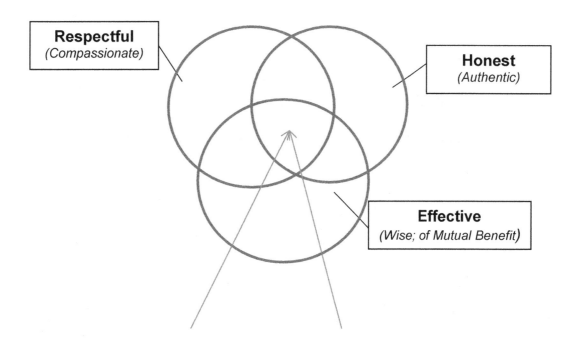

Listen for and *speak FEND*:

Facts (what was seen/heard)

Emotions (e.g., mad, sad, scared, glad)

Needs (e.g., connecting, creating, contributing)

Designs expressed as Requests

Practice the *Five P's*

Posture (internal; external)

Pause (to relax & re-center)

Ponder (e.g., feelings & needs)

Paraphrase (in your own words)

Pop the question
("Have I understood you correctly?")

SUGGESTED READING

Mindfulness & Empathy

Avram Davis, ed. *Meditation from the Heart of Judaism.*

Gefen, Nan Fink. *Discovering Jewish Meditation.*

Lew, Alan. *Be Still and Get Going.*

Rosenberg, Larry. *Three Steps to Awakening.*

Roth, Jeff. *Jewish Meditation Practices for Everyday Life.*

Salzberg, Sharon. *Real Happiness: The Power of Meditation—A 28-day Program.*

Slater, Jonathan. *Mindful Jewish Living.*

LifeView

Albom, Mitch. *Tuesdays with Morrie.*

Boorstein, Sylvia. *That's Funny, You Don't Look Buddhist.*

Cooper, David. *God is a Verb.*

Lew, Alan. *One God Clapping: The Spiritual Path of a Zen Rabbi.*

Morinis, Alan. *Climbing Jacob's Ladder.*

———. *Everyday Holiness.*

Shapiro, Rami. *Lovingkindness.*

Telushkin, Joseph. *Hillel: If Not Now, When?*

Compassionate Authenticity

Brown, Brené. *Rising Strong.*

Rosenberg, Marshall. *Nonviolent Communication.*

———. *Speak Peace in a World of Conflict.*

Telushkin, Joseph. *Words that Hurt, Words that Heal.*

INDEX

Acknowledgements

I want to express my gratitude to Marshall Rosenberg, the founder of Nonviolent Communication. I am also indebted to my mindfulness teachers, S.N. Goenka, Thich Nhat Hanh, and Larry Rosenberg. All four teachers have inspired me to work diligently to grow in the ability to engage and mediate conflict with mindfulness, empathy, and compassionate authenticity. Most of all, I am very grateful to my wife, Bess, for her loving companionship over the past 40 years; and to our daughter, Amanda, who gives me hope for the future. Thank you!

About the Author

Barry Nobel practiced family mediation for more than two decades and taught at the University of Oregon School of Law, Portland State University, Linfield College, the University of Puget Sound, the University of California, Santa Barbara, the Santa Barbara College of Law, and Lane Community College. Previously, he practiced law, coordinated a pro bono legal program, served as judicial clerk in the United States District Court, and published a local sports newspaper. Barry received a BA in Religion from Princeton University, a JD from the University of Oregon, and a PhD in Religious Studies from the University of California, Santa Barbara. He lives with his wife, Bess, in Oregon, near their daughter, Amanda, her husband, Sean, and grandson, Quinn. Barry and Bess enjoy traveling our beautiful and imperiled natural world in their vintage trailer. They welcome the opportunity to visit new places and offer workshops in Jewish approaches to mindfulness and mindfulness-based conflict engagement.

Made in the USA
Columbia, SC
31 July 2018